family living

family living

creating the
perfect family home

Judith Wilson

photography by Debi Treloar

RYLAND
PETERS
& SMALL
LONDON NEW YORK

First published in the United States in 2003
by Ryland Peters & Small
519 Broadway
Fifth Floor
New York, NY 10012
www.rylandpeters.com

10 9 8 7 6 5 4 3 2 1

ISBN 1 84172 406 8

Library of Congress Cataloging-in-Publication Data

Wilson, Judith, 1962-
  Family living : creating the perfect family home / by
Judith Wilson ; with photography by Debi Treloar.
     p. cm.
  ISBN 1-84172-406-8
  1. Interior decoration. I. Treloar, Debi. II. Title.
  NK2115 .W8154 2003
  747--dc21

                        2002015784

Designer Fiona Walker
Commissioning editor Annabel Morgan
Location research Judith Wilson and
Claire Hector
Production Patricia Harrington
Art director Gabriella Le Grazie
Publishing director Alison Starling

Stylist Judith Wilson

contents

introduction

Nothing beats family living. Chaotic and noisy it may be, but it's also sociable, fun, relaxing, and hilarious. For parents and kids alike, there's incalculable merit to a home where everyone can gather *en famille* or invite friends over for an impromptu supper. Lots of space, though always a bonus, is not the issue. Creating the perfect family home is about maximizing the potential of the space you already have.

The presence of kids demands long-term planning. Children canter through developmental phases, and swiftly graduate from needing kitchen-floor space to a bedroom hideaway. The key is flexibility, allowing room functions to be switched with minimal hassle. Plan for that, and the need for serial moving is reduced. It makes financial sense to create a home to grow into, and kids will appreciate the continuity.

Spatially speaking, this book is matched to the ebb and flow of real family life. Part One is about creating free-flowing activity zones. Part Two accepts that parents and kids both need time out, so it concerns peaceful zones. And, as every parent knows, a family home only works like clockwork if it's well-organized and practical, so Part Three sorts surfaces, storage, and spaces in between.

No family home should be a show home—after all, it's children's clutter that creates its true soul—but it shouldn't be a mess either. Enjoy creating a welcoming, beautiful, even sophisticated living space, and your kids will respect it and enjoy sharing it with you. And never underestimate the emotional power of the childhood home. Make it a fun place to be now, and your children will keep on returning long after they've flown the nest.

multifunctional kitchens
communal living rooms
playrooms and media rooms

activity zones

"Our kitchen is a very sociable space and the core of the home where everyone meets."

JEMIMA, AGE 17

"What matters is that we are all together as one unit, even if I'm cooking, my son is watching TV, and the baby is on the floor."

KATE, MOTHER

"We like the idea of a space role-reversal: an indoor space where kids can do outdoor things—rope-climbing, cycling—and an outdoors where we can eat and entertain."

HIRO, FATHER

multifunctional kitchens

Modern-day family life revolves around the kitchen. Hungry kids always make a beeline for it, and it's the focal point for family meals. The best-planned kitchens also provide a welcoming environment where children will want to study, watch television, and chat with their friends or (you never know) their parents. So create an open-plan, bright, yet functional space where everyone, including little ones, can enjoy sociable family living.

BELOW: Even in a small kitchen, try to provide several seating choices, from a formal dining table to a breakfast bar. On a daily basis, kids have more room to spread out with homework on one tabletop, while supper is laid on another. There's also twice the chair space for larger family gatherings. For a cohesive look, pick matching chair and stool styles.

RIGHT: When designing an island unit that doubles as a breakfast bar, make sure there's enough leg room under the counter for adults as well as kids, and that stools will tuck underneath, so small children won't crash into them.

LEFT: An island unit is the most sociable and useful component in a family kitchen. Perfect as a food preparation area or breakfast bar, or for dishing up food, islands work best when positioned centrally, dividing eating and cooking areas. Yet they can easily become a dumping ground for school books or last night's supper tray, so be strict about keeping the top clear. BELOW: During a typical weekend, families can get through an alarming number of glasses and dishes, so make life easy by amassing a generous selection. Open shelves, positioned close to the dishwasher, make all that unloading and table-laying much easier.

The whole point about creating a multifunctional space is that it provides room for cooking, eating, and living areas—all together. The advantages are obvious. Not only is there more room for kids to gather, so they are less likely to disappear upstairs, but if everyone wants to do something different (as is common in larger families), varying needs can be accommodated. Little ones can scoot around on tricycles, adults can cook, and homework can get underway.

Given that the kitchen is the nerve-center of the family home, it should be in an accessible location. Close to the front door makes for quick school exits, toast in hand, while a rear kitchen with backyard access is great for smaller children. In loft spaces or one-level apartments, a centrally situated open-plan kitchen is more sociable than a conventional galley at the end of a corridor. And in a house, make the kitchen the heart of the home by placing it right by the back door. If the kitchen is easy to get to, kids will be more likely to linger, long after their hunger pangs are satisfied.

THIS PAGE: When kids are little and play regularly in the kitchen, plan enough cabinets to accommodate their needs as well as storing cooking equipment. Low-level storage makes it easy for them to reach everything from art materials to videos. Plenty of drawers, with easy-to-grab handles, are often more helpful for organizing than deep cupboards.

OPPOSITE: In an open-plan multifunctional kitchen, use a choice of surfaces to delineate different activity areas. Here, wood veneer sections off the dining area, while painted doors indicate storage and a powder room.

THIS PAGE AND OPPOSITE, ABOVE: Custommade carpentry means even a narrow room can hold a dining table, seating bench, and food preparation zones. Essential appliances can be fitted into an island unit, and wall cupboards extended up to the ceiling. OPPOSITE, BELOW: Kids and adults alike will appreciate funky touches such as glitter mosaic tiles or a glass worktop with colorful under-counter lighting.

If you're adapting an existing property and the kitchen is inconveniently sited, consider relocating it. What may seem an extravagant option can be a sound investment if it makes the difference between staying put or moving as your family's needs change or expand. Try to use an architect (if funds are limited, many will work on a consultancy-only basis, providing ideas and drawings), but choose one familiar with family life, so the emphasis is on great space, not just designer statements.

If the kitchen is too small to incorporate additional living space, knocking through into an adjacent room or hallway can be one solution. If it's not an option to move existing kitchen cabinets, removing the upper part of the wall between the kitchen and living area will create a sociable connection. Even installing double doors to link the kitchen with the living room will make a vast difference.

When searching for a family home, make a big kitchen a top priority. Trendy city-dwellers are exploring not only lofts, but also commercial buildings such as garages and workshops, which offer extensive living space. New-build family homes are a brilliant option, providing the chance to truly redefine family living spaces. Older homes often have large kitchens, living rooms, and dining rooms that can be combined into open-plan living quarters, and many have the added advantage of a big yard.

When planning a kitchen, think in terms of free-flowing zones, rather than having conventional kitchen cabinets at one end of the room and a dining table at the other. Blurring the boundaries maximizes the available space. For example, a kitchen island unit could double as a breakfast bar, which obviates the need for a separate table (and is perfect for snacking kids). And placing all cupboards or units along one wall, rather than in a traditional L- or U-shape, means more floor space is freed up for little ones to run around. A single bank of wall cabinets designed to hold not just kitchen equipment and tableware, but toys and books as well will save on space and provide a more cohesive look to the room.

The best family kitchens boast efficient, capacious appliances. A dishwasher is essential, but think not just in terms of a large one (multiple guests for Sunday lunch), but also a quiet model that won't

ABOVE: In a new-build home or modern extension, a kitchen will become truly multifunctional if it is designed to lead directly to outdoor space, linked with floor-to-ceiling sliding glass doors. While small kids benefit from extra play space, grown-ups or teenagers can entertain inside or out.

OPPOSITE: A cutting-edge contemporary kitchen can still be family-friendly, when materials are carefully chosen. With its wipe-clean leather chairs, durable limestone floor, and hardwearing professional-style stainless-steel counters, this kitchen is practical by day, and sleek and sophisticated at night.

disturb post-supper television viewing. A built-in double oven or a freestanding industrial-style range will cater for large numbers, but team it with a microwave—essential for late-night teenage snacks. A six- rather than four-burner cooktop is very helpful. Also consider a big fridge-freezer, combined with an extra freezer (stored in a garage or cellar) for large-capacity food supplies.

Plan the cooking zone layout with you and the kids in mind, so it's easy for them to help with food preparation. Little ones love to bake with adults, while older children enjoy the independence of creating box lunches and simple meals. Consider a kitchen with under-the-counter cupboards only, so children can reach utensils with ease. Freestanding kitchen work stations and island units, accessible from all sides, are also child-friendly. A fridge at floor-level and a countertop microwave are safer than those built in at adult eye-level.

In a space where cooking and relaxing zones merge, plan for the inevitable messy, post-cooking kitchen. An island unit with a higher wall on the living side can bisect work and play areas, neatly

concealing kitchen clutter. In a loft space, a centrally sited kitchen zone can be screened off with wall-to-floor sliding composite or sand-blasted glass doors. If you are creating a new open-plan space, retain a slim section of wall to divide cooking and relaxing areas. Put kitchen storage cabinets on one side, and an inset TV and a giant pinboard on the other. And install a good extractor fan, so cooking smells don't stray to the rest of the house.

In decorative terms, the family kitchen should tread a fine line between looking cozy (for small children), stylish (for grown-up dinner parties), and a little bit funky (for teenagers). It must also be practical. That's not impossible to achieve. What matters most (as a good kitchen should last a decade plus), is that the essential bones—flooring, cupboard fronts, countertops—are classic and plain. Furniture and accessories can be matched to your kids' ages, tastes, and needs as these evolve. For example, a plain white kitchen might be accessorized first with pink mini chairs and table, swiftly followed by sociable wooden benches and gold glitter splashback tiles.

OPPOSITE, BELOW LEFT: Family life is busy enough without endlessly cleaning the kitchen, so pick easy-care surfaces. Stainless steel, glass, or stone can all be wiped clean. Alternatively, use tiles, from bright mosaics to hand-thrown ceramics, to inject a burst of strong color.

OPPOSITE, BELOW RIGHT: Casual robust furniture is the sensible option. Antique wood refectory or marble-topped bakery styles, or a zinc-topped thrift-store find make unusual yet relaxed choices, especially when teamed with mismatched wood or metal café chairs.

RIGHT AND BELOW: Faced with a very large open-plan multifunctional kitchen, such as in a loft space, it can be tempting to "fill" the space by dividing it into eating, cooking, and living zones. More usefully, plan to retain a generous amount of open floor space (perfect for parties, as well as small kids running around), then group all the activity zones close together for intimacy and practicality. Grown-ups don't want to carry hot dishes far from stove to dining table, and kids like perching on a chair close enough to chat to parents preparing food.

LEFT: Efficiency is all-important in the kitchen, so even if the room is small, it makes sense to incorporate generously sized appliances and compromise on storage. Pans and plates can be stacked on open shelves, but a full-size dishwasher is an absolute essential.

BELOW AND OPPOSITE: In a corridor-style kitchen, even the smallest table makes the room user-friendly for kids, too. If there's no space for a freestanding piece, consider a built-in tabletop squeezed into an alcove with stools neatly tucked beneath.

Do use color in the kitchen. Children respond instinctively to it and will find a kitchen with a tangerine-painted wall or leaf-green rubber floor much more fun to spend time in. Color also lends instant atmosphere. If you're a white-and-stainless-steel fan, think instead of using colorful accessories. Cheerful shades may also help to "zone" the areas within a very large space.

When kids are around, it pays to choose practical, wipe-clean cabinet doors. For trendy minimalists, white or colored laminates, stainless steel, sand-blasted glass, and spray-painted board are all great door options. A more classic look, as good with country as with trendy furniture, is achieved with painted tongue-and-groove or paneled wood. Invest in a quality work surface, since it needs to withstand lots of wear and tear. Stainless steel and solid wood look all the better for a few scuffs, while granite and marble provide a sleeker finish. And Corian, while expensive, is incredibly hard-wearing and comes in myriad colors. Less costly options include concrete and laminates.

OPPOSITE: If your family is large and space isn't a problem, a generously proportioned table and matching benches provides a sociable and practical seating option. Most dining tables are a standard size, so consider commissioning a scaled-up table from a local furniture maker.

LEFT: In a big multifunctional space, it's essential to think about heating. No-one will gather in the kitchen if it's draughty or chilly. Consider underfloor heating, big cast-iron radiators, or modern options such as floor-level cylinder styles.

The kitchen floor must be robust. This is the heaviest traffic area of the house and the floor will need to withstand food spills, riotous games, and muddy feet. Solid wood flooring may prove more enduring than some wood laminates. Consider reclaimed boards or painted floorboards, which are easy to touch up. Stone and painted concrete are hard-wearing options, but more sensible for small children are linoleum or rubber, which come in fabulous bright colors. Also check out unusual choices, such as squash-court flooring, which is springy underfoot.

Great storage is vital in a family kitchen. First, there's the basic cooking gear, with multiple pots and pans. Seasoned parents also know that bottle sterilizers and the baby mouli soon give way to extensive bakeware (from muffin to birthday-cake pans) and popsicle molds, not to mention all those appliances, from ice-cream makers to espresso machines. Plenty of deep drawers, rather than cabinets, often make for the easiest access, though locate frequently used appliances on the countertop.

When a kitchen constitutes the main living space, there must also be storage for leisure materials, from board games to paints. The neatest solution is to match cupboards to kitchen units. If the kitchen is not built-in, go for open shelves lined with rows of identical labeled boxes (rattan, cardboard, or metal) or a quirky, thrift-store armoire equipped with labeled containers of varying sizes, to help kids (and you) stay organized.

Tableware also needs a home. Even a small family should have double or triple quantities of everything. Locate everything near the dining area, and keep everyday stuff down low so little ones can help set the table. To suit classic kitchens, a distressed wooden hutch is a great storage option; in trendier homes, stash everything in sleek floor-to-ceiling cupboards or a stylish sideboard. What about good family tableware? A robust set of white tableware is an excellent start. To this, add jolly colored glasses, patterned bowls, and trendy tablemats. Younger children will also enjoy personalizing the table with numbered napkin rings or monogrammed cups.

Shared mealtimes are crucial to family life, so while a breakfast bar is great for quick meals, make sure there is a table aand enough seating for everyone to sit down together. Get as big a dining table as possible, preferably an extending one

(a round table is good for smaller spaces). Since the table will be used alternately for homework, model-making, or daily paperwork, choose one with a hard-wearing surface, so there's no need for a protective cloth. Solid wood, stainless steel or zinc, laminates and painted composite board are all ideal.

The best seating options allow for extra guests at a moment's notice. Children enjoy squashing onto wooden benches or a built-in banquette upholstered in wipe-clean leather or vinyl. Stools are cool for teenagers, from traditional laboratory ones to modern classics in metal. It's a good idea to choose stacking or folding chairs so extras are easily stored—go for plastic, metal, or wood, and save upholstery for the empty-nest years!

In a multizoned space, plan your lighting carefully. While cooking and play zones should have excellent low-voltage overhead lighting, the dining area needs a decorative hanging

OPPOSITE: Cheerful color is essential if the family kitchen is to be welcoming. In addition to painting the walls, consider colored laminate counters, painted units, and bright tiles. Colored surfaces are less likely to show up scuffs than pristine white ones.

ABOVE LEFT: The kitchen is the ideal space to show off children's art, be it splashes of paint or a teenage masterpiece.
ABOVE RIGHT AND BELOW: When space is tight, an upholstered banquette can double up as comfy seating for dinner and a television-watching sofa.

light fixture, preferably on a dimmer switch so you can set the right tone for dinner parties or use the light turned right up as task lighting for homework.

If space permits, it's great to have a comfy zone in the kitchen, even if you have a den, too. Small two-seater sofas, bean bags, or a daybed take up minimal room, and add splashes of jolly color if sensibly slipcovered in bright cotton or a funky retro print. Combine any of these with a low-level television, built into a storage unit, inset in an alcove, or wall-mounted on an extending bracket so it can be viewed from the cooking zone, too. And don't forget music. Whether it's nursery rhymes or hip hop, everyone should be able to dance in the kitchen. So a good sound system, with concealed or wall-mounted speakers, is essential, especially for parties. And while sorting technology, don't forget phone jacks for the telephone and the laptop.

However well-planned, a multifunctional space only works at full capacity if organization is spot-on. Keep track of school activities and artwork by providing a large pinboard or painting a section of wall with magnetic paint. Add a whiteboard so everyone takes responsibility for relaying phone messages and shopping lists. And don't forget a large clock, so being late for school—or breaking the curfew—is never an option!

OPPOSITE: The family kitchen is for grown-ups to enjoy as well as children, so avid cooks should choose a casual style with all their utensils nearby. Not only will this encourage budding foodies, but there's less pressure to clear up than in a minimalist-style room.
LEFT: Kitchen eating is about casual entertaining, but plan your accessories so the dining table can look formal on special occasions. Pick easy-wash tablecloths, from rough antique linens to a denim table runner that won't stain if red grape juice (or red wine) gets spilled.

communal living rooms

The best family living rooms are cozy enough for lazy Sunday afternoons, and chic enough for grown-up entertaining. A flexible furniture layout helps accommodate larger numbers on high days and holidays. Don't make the living room a no-go zone for younger children. Choose practical furnishings that everyone can enjoy without worrying about spills. Textures should be warming and touchy-feely, from fluffy throws to a soft rug underfoot.

BELOW LEFT AND RIGHT: Personalize the living room with decorative finds—even little children appreciate pretty things, and jewel-colored velvet cushions, a twinkling chandelier, or a giant canvas will appeal to kids and adults alike. Place anything breakable out of reach until the later years, and for practicality, choose shabby chic over precious antiques. Counter grown-up choices with easy-care whitewashed floorboards and washable slipcovers. OPPOSITE: Don't automatically rule out enjoying serious contemporary art. Children will enjoy the stimulation of colorfully hung walls and find their own "pictures" within abstract displays.

Even if much of the family's weekday activity is kitchen-based, if space permits, it's great to have a separate living room. In the evenings, parents of small children will enjoy a toy-free zone, and older kids will also appreciate a quiet spot to escape to. It's helpful for kids to learn the difference between a sophisticated entertaining space and kitchen living—they are easily taught to respect nice things. Make rules early on, then don't nag. You don't want cupcakes on the sofa, but there's nothing wrong with the pop-up tent if it means everyone is together.

Think about your living room. Does its location fit the lifestyle and ages of your children? With little ones, it's a boon to have one close to the kitchen, so you can keep track of who's up to what. With teenagers, an upstairs living room might put a peaceful distance between you and their friends. Do you use the space to its best advantage? Many families have a formal room for special occasions, but avoid it like the plague. If this is you, ask yourself why? Is the room dark, is it too big or too cold?

THIS PAGE: It's a fact of family life that most kids sprawl on the floor. Make it cozy with a sheepskin or fluffy deep-pile wool rug, and add character with a contemporary design, choosing from candy-spotted styles to abstract squiggles or *faux animal skins.*

OPPOSITE, ABOVE: Furnish each chair with a side table, so there's less likelihood of drinks getting spilled.

OPPOSITE, BELOW LEFT AND RIGHT: In a contemporary living room, tailormade wall-mounted storage can hold everything from videos to family photos.

Often the best solution is to swap rooms around. Perhaps a dingy room could be converted into a media room, while a sunny bedroom does service as a living room instead?

Consider who will use the living room daily, what numbers are likely to swell to on weekends, and what activities will take place there? In addition to the inevitable socializing, there will probably be television viewing and family games. Ask your older children how they anticipate using the room. Once you've got the answers, the space can be zoned accordingly. In L-shaped or long, narrow living rooms, it's useful to bisect the space into a main social area with a reading zone at the other end. A very large room might be divided with double doors, with the stereo in one, the TV in the other, thus controlling dual noise sources.

Decide on the room's natural focus. If it's the television, accept the fact with good grace and arrange the furniture accordingly. Choose a contemporary television on a stand, and put it center stage instead of trying to conceal it in a cabinet.

OPPOSITE: The best family living rooms are full of cozy personal memorabilia. Frame family photos simply, then make a decorative, ever-changing feature of them by propping them casually on several shelves. Let the kids have the freedom to add and take away as new ones appear. LEFT AND RIGHT: Even in a busy family home, it's still possible to enjoy the versatility and sophistication of that eternal living room classic—the white armchair. Practical options include preshrunk washable cotton, muslin, linen/cotton blends, or denim made into slipcovers, or wipe-clean white leather or vinyl.

A fireplace also creates a wonderful focus. A real fire, or gas-effect log one, can do wonders in winter to tempt antisocial teenagers downstairs, and there's nothing quite like gathering around it for making home seem a cozy place to be. When little ones are around, use a fireguard and keep matches well out of the way.

Decoratively speaking, start with surfaces. Aim to create a relaxed and cozy visual tone, appealing to grown-ups and kids alike. Good soft colors include dusty pinks and neutrals, from mushroom to biscuit, or warming shades like terracotta. With small kids around, painted walls are easy to touch up, while patterned wallpapers or textured finishes are excellent for concealing little fingerprints. Children naturally gravitate downward, so they will beg for soft flooring. Either choose neutral carpeting—100 percent wool, so it cleans easily—or wooden floorboards. Add a rug that can be rolled up for parties. Don't choose sisal; it's too scratchy to lie on.

Great seating is crucial. There should be a comfortable spot for every member of the family, plus spare for visiting friends. If your children are still little, often the best option is a vast three-seater sofa, so the whole family can cuddle up together. Older (and bigger) kids

LEFT: If there is space, some families prefer the option of a formal living room for grown-up entertaining, combined with a cozy den for TV-watching on week nights. But don't opt for sophisticated finishes at the expense of banning the kids entirely—they should still be able to pile in on high days and holidays. The ideal mix is chic furniture outlines—streamlined oblong sofas, curvy occasional chairs—combined with upholstery in sensible dark shades, so marks won't show.
BELOW AND OPPOSITE: Always include some occasional or modular seating that is easy to move around—from upholstered cubes to a single armchair—so impromptu quiet corners are easily arranged.

might prefer two smaller sofas, placed sociably opposite one another, plus assorted armchairs, or an L-shaped modular seating unit. For teenagers—or weary adults—a daybed is perfect for lounging, as is a large upholstered stool on castors for small kids. The more pieces of furniture you can have on wheels, the better, so for larger social gatherings, floor space is easily cleared.

Upholstery fabrics must be practical, because all the food rules in the world won't prevent the inevitable spills. But you can still have attractive, beautiful textiles. Good upholstery options include wool bouclé or wool blends, chenille, or velvet. Pick them in deep, rich shades and they won't show marks: deep purple, charcoal, and berry tones are all trendy, pretty choices. If you're after muted, pale colors, white or pastel upholstery is still an option, but opt for slipcovers in washable fabric such as preshrunk denim. Leather and vinyl, in brown, black, or white, are truly sensible choices.

Children love fun, versatile seating. They particularly enjoy low-level options that can be pulled up to a coffee table for an afternoon snack, or for television watching. Consider beanbags or seating cubes, which look very sophisticated in leather or felt. Also include at least one chair that affords privacy for reading: a wing chair, rocking chair, or a modern-day classic like the Egg swivel chair. Children love the novelty of a frivolous piece of furniture. If your style is traditional, why not upholster one piece in a bright color—a scarlet armchair, say—or look for a funky retro swivel chair if your room is contemporary.

Where possible, pick occasional furniture with a dual function, to save space and cater for varied demands. A big coffee table is useful for multiple teenage coffee cups as well as providing a base for board games, but pick one with shelf storage beneath for stacks of comics and books. A Sixties-style low sideboard offers great display space on top and can hold an entire family's photo albums and video collection. It's also nice to have a permanently set-up table, with dining chairs, for a jigsaw in progress or adult card games. Whatever the furniture, go for

OPPOSITE: If there's no space for a separate formal living room, it's still possible to engineer a relaxed ambient mood in a communal living area, even if it leads directly off the kitchen. Mark the difference between the two areas by choosing the occasional piece of curvaceous furniture, from a deep swivel chair to an antique armoire, a round coffee table to a chandelier. Practicality still matters: these armoires, for example, hold toys and tableware.
THIS PAGE: When kids are young, furnish the living area sparsely, so there's plenty of central floor space for the sprawling out and endless game playing.

pieces in robust materials like wood or painted board, rather than plastic (which will scratch) or glass (too many sharp corners). Distressed secondhand antiques, rather than rare and precious ones, are also preferable. If smaller children are around, think about safety. Tiny occasional tables can go flying, as can floor lamps and floor-standing glass vases.

Every living room needs storage. Make a list of what needs to live here, from books and videos to photo albums and board games. For the most serene mood, pick storage with doors that conceal clutter. If the room is contemporary, consider a freestanding cabinet or flush wall units, or if traditional, a bureau teamed with paneled alcove cupboards. Help kids keep things neat by filling each piece of storage with smaller labeled boxes. Books are essential in the living room, providing stimulus for children and creating instant ambience for everyone.

OPPOSITE, ABOVE, AND BELOW: In a one-level apartment, or a double drawing room where two rooms have been knocked into one, combining a comfortable living area with a dining room is a sociable arrangement. Grown-ups can chat over dinner, while the kids chill out with the TV. It's vital to be able to separate each area, so double doors or sliding screens should be installed. THIS PAGE: Alternatively, you could plan a more formal seating arrangement at one end of the room and a cozy area at the other, complete with squashy armchairs and wall-to-wall books, videos, magazines, and CDs.

Consider built-in shelves in an alcove, a wall of contemporary, thick-fronted shelves, or a freestanding bookcase. Whatever the style, position the kids' books on lower shelves for easy access.

When choosing accessories for the living room, don't forget this is the kids' space, too. Children will respond to an overly formal, pared-down room by refusing to sit in it—it's that simple. So ask them which precious things they would like to include. Great choices include "found" objects picked up on a family vacation, from shells to a twisted piece of driftwood, or a child's artwork, beautifully framed. The living room is also the place for family photos. Tuck them into an overmantel mirror or have them framed to fill a whole wall. Kids, as well as visitors, will enjoy a collage of photos of parents, grandparents, babies, and kids. You could commission a portrait of your kids—the most personal artwork of all.

The living room is for relaxing in, so make it comfortable. Small children are tactile creatures and love to cocoon themselves in something soft while winding down before bed. Teenagers will do the same. Furnish sofas with plump feather-filled cushions in touchy-feely textiles like velvet and mohair. Always have a few throws on hand, in something cozy like ribbed wool or chenille, and don't be precious about little ones using them, too. Finally, remember that kids—just like grown-ups—appreciate fresh flowers and delicious smells. Light a scented candle spiked with fig or vanilla, and every seat in the room will be occupied in twenty seconds flat.

OPPOSITE AND LEFT: It's impossible to create a formal living area in an open-plan space where a kitchen table or play area are also visible. Instead, go for a colorful, relaxed bohemian look. Kids love this laidback style, because a little mess doesn't matter, and for grown-ups, with the lights down low and the fire lit, it creates an atmospheric space for more formal adult entertaining.

playrooms and media rooms

Kids love a designated playroom where they can keep their toys and play with friends. And grown-ups like them, too, because they can shut a door on the mess! As children grow up, a properly planned playroom can easily evolve into a media room or teenage den. So furnish it first with great storage, practical surfaces, and enough technology to cope with media leisure. Add cozy seating, and grown-ups will want to chill out in there, too.

A designated playroom helps contain the sea of paraphernalia that comes with kids. There are doll buggies and sit-on cars, then sports gear and art materials, not to mention the piano or football table. For parents, it can be a relief that these won't stray all over the house, and for children it's nice not to have to put away games in progress every night. It's also comforting for children to have a space they can call their own, particularly if bedrooms are shared. Later on, furnished with a desk and computer, a playroom becomes a place for homework. For older families, a home entertainment, or media room, is an increasingly popular option. In here, everything from the television and DVD player to the stereo system and Playstation can be stylishly concealed and easily accessed.

Family homes rarely have rooms to spare, but however short of space you are, it's worth considering whether room functions can be switched. A designated den makes for more spacious,

LEFT AND OPPOSITE ABOVE: In a relaxed live/play space, younger kids will appreciate fun extras like a swing or punchbag, or foldaway equipment like an easel or teepee. Install them beside the main traffic area, with cushions and a rug close by.
OPPOSITE BELOW: Allocate a separate tabletop or shelf to the kids, so drawing or homework needn't be cleared away when supper is ready. Overhead storage, or baskets clipped to one side, hold essentials.
BELOW: Experiment with novel ways to display kids' artworks, such as a wall-mounted clothes-line and wooden pins.

tranquil living quarters elsewhere. Could two children share a bedroom, freeing up space for a playroom? If the kitchen contains an eating zone, could the dining room become a media room? What about an attic conversion, or the cellar? A solarium extension is ideal for a playroom, because it is light and has outdoor access, as is a garden gazebo, wired and plumbed—perfect for noise control!

If a separate room isn't an option, try to demarcate a play or chill-out zone within the family living space. For tinies, allocate floor space within the kitchen (safely away from the cooking area) so you can keep a close eye on them. Older children might appreciate a nook for table football, a basketball hoop on an upstairs landing, or even a small climbing wall, for the very brave! Make the boundaries clear. In a contemporary kitchen, different-colored linoleum squares, a padded mattress, or gym mats could mark out the kids' space. Alternatively, use freestanding storage units to divide off an area. In open-plan apartments or lofts, a mini maze is lots of fun.

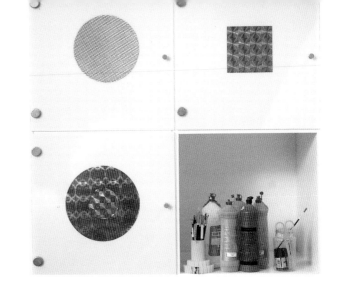

OPPOSITE: Get the best use out of a designated playroom by keeping storage streamlined to free up maximum floor space. If kids are musical, this is the place to keep the piano or drums. Also consider table football, snooker, or plastic play equipment, such as a toddler's kitchenette. The less furniture there is, the more useful the room is for impromptu parties.
LEFT: Don't feel constrained to keep everything child-sized, as the best dens will appeal to grown-ups, too. Choose squashy beanbags, a wall-size blackboard, or a big chill-out sofa.
ABOVE: Aim for easy-access storage, but put in a few doors so the worst mess can be instantly concealed.

OPPOSITE AND ABOVE: In a traditional playroom, keep things simple, with white walls and wooden floors, and let the toys—dolls' things, cars and trucks—create the decorative impact. Allow kids the creative freedom to display everything from their favorite paintings to postcards, memorabilia, or photos. Allocate wall space or special shelves or provide a few bowls for favorite things to be grouped together.

LEFT: Invest in a large armoire into which everything can be cleared away. It could also be wired to hold the playroom TV and video.

When decorating a designated playroom, approach it with a creative spirit and ask the kids what they'd like—after all, this is their space. Painted walls are practical, and it can be fun to have a wall or two in jolly colors the children have chosen. Look out for kids' paint lines, which include sparkly and magnetic paint options, and choose gloss paint for woodwork: it's easy to wipe down. Equip one wall with a metal board and magnets, and consider a large blackboard, or blackboard paint on cupboard fronts. Older children might like to customize their space. Provide them with a 2-yard-square canvas (from art suppliers) and let them paint it with their own design, to fill one wall.

In the playroom, as in the kitchen, practical flooring is essential to withstand games and messy play. Don't choose sisal, which is uncomfortable to lie on and hard to clean. Go for painted floorboards, rubber, or linoleum. The latter can be cut into myriad patterns, from camouflage print to abstract flowers.

While a playroom would be no fun without some scaled-down pieces of furniture, such as little tables and chairs, plan larger pieces with growing up in mind. Choose an adult-sized sofa and install built-in desktops on a rack system, so the level can be raised as children grow. Likewise, swivel desk chairs should be height-adjustable, particularly important as children sit for longer hours doing homework. Plan capacious storage that fills an entire wall, and teenagers will still be using it long after the

playroom has become a den. In a playroom, toy storage is all about instant access, so go for built-in shelves stacked with crates, or an open cube system. Flexible freestanding options include a map chest (good for storing artwork) or a television/video unit on wheels.

As kids get older, they (and you) might want more than just a television in the playroom. Today's family home is increasingly infiltrated by media of all types, including satellite television, computer games, and DVD players. It can make sense to devote an entire room to home entertainment. Options range from a trendy wall-mounted plasma-screen television to a motorized cinema screen for movies. There can be surround-sound emerging from concealed speakers, CD players, even a special socket so children can safely

LEFT: A playroom is the ideal spot for displaying family photos, sports trophies, or other memorabilia.
ABOVE AND BELOW: Keep furnishings ultra-practical, so that TV dinners or teenage nights in can take place with minimum fuss, and an upholstered stool won't wilt beneath muddy trainers. Leather, vinyl, or washable slipcovers are cozy yet practical choices.

plug in the Playstation. The beauty of such rooms is that all the technology is controlled by one automated operating system, hidden in a cupboard. It's not cheap to install, and you will need to decorate the room from scratch once the cabling is in place. But there are huge advantages. Teenagers can play loud music, or watch DVDs you'd rather not share, while you reclaim a tranquil living room. And, precisely because the technology must be installed by specialists, there will be no trailing cords and fewer television sets elsewhere in the house.

Decorate a media room with relaxation in mind. There should be enough seating to accommodate family and friends. Low-level daybeds or modular seating systems upholstered in denim, velvet, or chenille set the right tone, as do battered leather armchairs. Alternatively, consider floor-level seating like big floor cushions and a rug to sprawl on. Pay attention to lighting. If overhead low-voltage lights are necessary, add a dimmer switch, and try to include a fun, wall-mounted light. Don't forget a good task light, too, if the computer is located in here.

For successful viewing, a room needs good light control. Cover windows with blackout blinds and play up the mood with deep wall colors, from caramel to olive. Alternatively, experiment with fabric-covered walls, which are good for light and noise control. If the room is predominantly for teenagers, make it fun for them. Choose large-scale mural wallpaper—an alpine scene or enlarged graphic images—or sparkly wallpaper. Make the media room a funky hideaway, and whatever's on, everyone will be in there watching.

LEFT, ABOVE AND BELOW: Position the television according to the ages of your family. Kids love sprawling on the floor, so choose a TV on an adjustable stand, set into a fireplace or—if choosing a plasma screen—wall-mounted at a low level. Have fun with media room furnishings, as kids and adults alike enjoy splashes of bright colors, either as rugs, cushions, or upholstery.

kids' rooms

shared bathrooms

parents' rooms

peaceful zones

"It's so important for a child to be able to shut his or her bedroom door and have solitude. Younger children need that for imaginative play, and privacy is even more important for teenagers."

KATE, MOTHER

"It's good to have my own room—a place where I can take my friends, away from everyone else, and listen to music."

JOSH, AGE 15

"Our bathroom has a huge Japanese-style bath, so we bathe together—it's both meditative and fun."

CECILIE, MOTHER

kids' rooms

From babyhood to the teenage years, a child's room is a tranquil retreat, somewhere to sleep and dream. Respect your children's need for privacy and quiet. Remember, too, that for kids, a bedroom represents the one space they can truly make their own, filled with all their favorite things. While young ones need a watchful decorative eye, allow teenagers flexibility. Let them experiment and make mistakes—they have to sleep in there, not you!

When family living space is properly planned, with storage equally distributed around the house, the kids' rooms will benefit, too. Instead of battling with clutter, you (and they) have the chance to create a personalized area where kids feel relaxed playing or entertaining their friends. Children's lives are busier than ever, so it's essential to help them wind down at night. For younger ones, the answer is to keep computers and televisions out of the bedroom. For teenagers (who may insist on them), concentrate instead on promoting a relaxed ambience. Whatever the age, remember that the best bedrooms provide a truly peaceful place to sleep.

If you have several children, allocate bedrooms fairly, as size does matter. Babies will be happy in a small cozy room, and teenagers won't mind either, tending to value privacy over square feet. It's in the middle years that children will benefit from greater floor space, so their room can double as a playroom. Consider location. Tinies will gain comfort from sleeping right next to the master bedroom (and you will appreciate a shorter trip in the middle of the night). By contrast, older kids will positively prefer a corridor between you and them, or even sleeping on another floor. An attic hideaway is the best noise-control solution for teenage music-lovers.

Before considering the decor, plan the storage space, as no child will be able to sleep peacefully if there's mess all over the floor. For flexibility, combine a variety of different options. Built-in cupboards, with plenty of adjustable shelves, are ideal, but also provide some open shelves, for books and displaying treasures. Sturdy hooks, with some hangers, are essential, so

OPPOSITE: When they are little, same-sex siblings may prefer sharing a low double bed, with two covers, rather than beds at opposite ends of the room. Or consider two divans, side by side, which can be separated to give independence in later years.

ABOVE RIGHT: Combine proper closet storage with easy-access shelves, so toddlers can find their favorite things.
RIGHT: Lighting is crucial. Cover windows with blinds or curtains lined with blackout material, and put overhead lights on a dimmer switch.

RIGHT AND OPPOSITE: A custom-built bed maximizes space in a small room and adds quirky charm. And little children are less likely to fall out of beds that are boxed in (opposite) or have high sides. Sketch a style or amass tear-sheets, then get a carpenter to build a simple frame and paint it in a jolly shade. Storage can be incorporated in the form of underbed drawers, or consider a platform bed with low cupboards beneath. Younger children will always appreciate a bed tucked against the wall or into a corner for added security.

busy kids can hang up clothes quickly if they don't make it to the closet. Teenagers may prefer a chrome, shop-style hanging rack or a low, denim-covered storage unit in place of a chest of drawers. Kids of every age need easy-access floor-level storage, from plastic crates on castors to metal cans, so shoes and toys can be quickly sorted out and put away.

For babies, the bedroom should be styled as simply as possible. This not only guarantees a tranquil space for sleep, but allows for the child to slowly grow into the room, amassing possessions along the way. Even at the tiny baby stage, it pays to take a more long-term view when you are kitting out the bedroom. At first, the most essential piece is the crib, but within two years, along with the changing table, this will be redundant. In contrast, other key basics, including a chest of drawers, plenty of storage or shelves, and a comfortable feeding then reading chair, should last throughout a child's time at home. Look out for funky extras to please preschool toddlers, such as a miniature table and chairs or a blow-up armchair.

Decoratively speaking, it's fun to use color in a baby's room, so don't fret about choosing peaceful shades (a blackout blind is what really promotes sleep). For a contemporary look, try painting blocks of solid color on two walls, while keeping the others white, or spray-paint a built-in storage unit bright pink or orange. Wool carpet or rubber tiles in acid shades are an energizing, practical choice. If you're artistic, attempting a large-scale mural is fun, but pick a unisex theme, such as the rain forest, so it's suitable for siblings sharing later. Do use pattern, as little ones relish it. Steer clear of patterned wallpaper, which dates quickly, and pick printed bedlinen or pillows. They can be altered as tastes change. Whimsical prints, from animals to fruit, or abstracts, from dots to stripes, will please both sexes and endure beyond gimmicky kids' TV characters.

Small kids appreciate the fun of trendy, multifunctional furniture, so start with the bed. Always choose a full-size single bed, as kids quickly grow out of miniature styles. Bunk bed styles, in ready-to-paint wood or minimal tubular steel, are perennial favorites, perhaps because they double as a jungle gym! For girls, a simple wood or metal four-poster offers endless decorative opportunities—adorn it with voile curtains, strands of beads, or floral lights. A low divan on giant castors, with plenty of underbed storage, is another fun option. The beauty of dual-purpose furniture is that it's space-saving and grows up with your child. A platform bed with a tabletop, bookshelf, and chair slotted underneath will be perfect for homework in later years, while a built-in alcove bed can be transformed into a grown-up daybed for teeny-bop girls.

LEFT, ABOVE, AND BELOW: Many older children are enthusiastic collectors, be it of toy soldiers or plastic animals, so provide plenty of display space. Wall-mounted shelves or a low work surface are good choices, but consider a paneled closet with chicken wire instead of glass, or a series of wall-mounted boxes, into which everything from baby ballet shoes to dried leaves and pretty shells can be arranged.

OPPOSITE: Plan a child's work station with the same care you would devote to an adult home office. Aim to make it comfortable and inspiring, so kids actively want to spend time there. Brightly colored units, a flower-bedecked swivel chair, or a pinboard on the closet door are all popular additions. The child's desk should be positioned to obtain maximum benefit from natural light. Don't forget to install outlets for a good task light and computer, and a telephone line for the internet.
LEFT: If you have a playroom elsewhere in the house, keep things ultra-simple in a shared room, with barely more than a bed and adequate clothes storage.

Furniture needs alter radically at seven-plus. First, there's homework. Doing it at the kitchen table shouldn't be the only option: every child needs a quiet spot to study. Provide them with a roomy desk so they can spread out (or work with a friend) and a height-adjustable chair (or two), with a filing cabinet or storage crates beneath. Don't forget an internet phone jack if computer homework is likely. It's better to customize an adult work table than waste money on small kiddie-size desks. A built-in wooden countertop can be spray-painted in bright gloss, while a trestle table can be jazzed up with a trendy plastic swivel chair. If space permits, devote an entire wall to a purpose-built storage and desk unit, with cubbyholes for everything from CDs to books. Now's also the time to provide girls with a dresser, for all that sparkly jewelry, or boys with a low hobby table.

These days, children are so style-conscious that from three up, they'll want to have a say in decorative decisions. Provided you've chosen plain flooring and a simple white blackout window shade or Venetian blind, kids can customize and change their

THIS PAGE: Match kids' rooms stylistically to the rest of the house. If you prefer antique or thrift-store styles, have fun searching for quirky furniture children will enjoy, too. Fun bed choices include *bateau lits*, a Victorian iron four-poster, or a dormitory style. All will last a child into their late teens and can be made more grown-up with sophisticated bedlinen.

OPPOSITE: Give kids a chance to get into good grooming habits by supplying a dresser for girls or a chunky chest of drawers for boys, plus a mirror positioned low enough for them to use.

rooms with regularity. Windows can be hung with ready-made curtains, in any fabric from denim to lurex, and walls repainted in a fresh color each year, provided your children are handy with a paintbrush! Older kids may like to consider wallpapers specifically aimed at the preteen market, from raised glitter hearts to abstract circles.

Encourage children to mix patterns rather than using matching coordinates. On the bed, printed quilt covers, in patterns ranging from gingham to stylized flowers, can be teamed with fleece blankets in *faux* leopard or Mexican stripes. Look out for fun extras such as a camouflage pillow cover for boys or a satin-effect eiderdown for girls. There's a good reason for keeping pattern to accessories rather than emblazoned all over the walls or floor. In larger families, it's likely children will swap bedrooms or decide to share, then return to the original set-up. Personalize a bedroom too much, and that freedom is curtailed.

If kids share permanently, help them maintain privacy and create a small space of their own. Little ones will enjoy bunks or beds close together, but older children may prefer to sleep at opposite ends of a room, with a dividing partition.

ABOVE, LEFT TO RIGHT: Kids love to personalize their own bedrooms, and this is particularly crucial in a large family. Let them paint their names on the bedroom door, add a monogrammed pillow to each bed, or—in a shared room—individualize their space with a specific theme, from underwater to a sports motif.

RIGHT: Some girls will want to mark the transition from childhood to the teenage years by opting for a simple, plain space with a few funky accessories, but be warned—the all-white minimalist look only works for super-neat individuals.

OPPOSITE: Keep things simple for teenage boys, too. Easy-to-use underbed storage, a no-nonsense bed, and utility bedlinen, from camouflage prints to a striped wool blanket, will be appreciated.

Flexible freestanding options include a large bookcase or a wooden screen on castors. A permanent partition wall can be made more sociable if portholes are cut into it at intervals. Sliding doors dividing the two areas, perhaps painted with blackboard paint or covered with cork pinboards, also help personalize areas.

Don't panic when children hit the teenage years. The key is to hand over decorative responsibility to them (within limits!). Get them to plan a scheme on a budget—artistic individuals can sketch out the look, too. Try to be open-minded about color choice. No doubt boys will want to replace the cheerful brights of earlier years with moody navy and khaki, while girls will plump for bordello pink and black, but adolescents need to experiment and develop their tastes. Take them shopping for funky accessories, from velvet curtains to a wacky lampshade—this may be just the encouragement they need to make them proud of their space and keep it neat.

There is a solution to poster-splattered walls. Come to an agreement that one wall only can be decorated any way they like (from spray-can graffiti to Warhol-style repeat photocopies) while the rest remains plain and unadorned. Alternatively, put up a giant metal pinboard with lots of magnets, so poster images are artfully contained. In a converted attic space, bare concrete or brick walls will be deemed the ultimate in cool.

The average teen room also doubles as space for entertaining. If the room is tiny, a divan can be converted into a sophisticated daybed with the addition of a fitted cover and bolsters. If there's space, create a sitting area with vinyl pouffes or a foam mattress or futon, covered in hard-wearing denim— not only perfect for lounging on, but also useful for sleepovers. Invest in a few extras, such as a coffee table or a TV cabinet on wheels, and they'll never come downstairs again.

shared bathrooms

The family bathroom is one of the hardest-working rooms in the house. To cope with the endless stream of twice-daily ablutions, it needs excellent plumbing, a free-flowing layout, and as many wash options as possible, from double basins to a power shower. Yet it's essential to combine practicality and beauty. After all, for grown-ups, the bathroom must also be a place that visually and physically soothes at the end of a long, hard day.

More than ever, we're a nation obsessed with cleanliness. The family bathroom has to withstand the early morning rush, splashy kids' bath times, and the grown-ups' long, leisurely soak, not to mention teenagers endlessly sprucing themselves up in the shower. Plan the bathroom well, and there's less likelihood of that clichéd line outside the bathroom door.

We can't all have a huge bathroom, but with lots of people sharing, generous proportions do help. If there's only one tiny bathroom at home, consider moving it. This sounds a big upheaval, but relocating the bathroom to a larger room can be well worth the expense and effort. Less radically, could you knock through to an adjacent closet, or steal some space from a next-door bedroom? Sometimes, opting for one large bathroom with an additional small shower room is more functional than two tiny connecting bathrooms.

Think about location. If kids are small, it's essential that the bathroom is on the same level as their bedrooms, to make nighttime trips easier. Remember that plumbing can be noisy if you've installed

OPPOSITE: Plan streamlined storage so the bathroom isn't cluttered. A glass-fronted cabinet can be inset into the wall—with its "invisible" frontage, it's less likely to attract small children's attention if medicines are stored inside. Wall-mounted basins, with towel holders below, are also helpful.

ABOVE: A shower can be incorporated into a family bathroom by stealing space at one end of the room and concealing it behind an internal wall.
BELOW: Innovative ways to link a bathroom to the master bedroom include a window-style opening, (with shutters for privacy), or sliding or folding doors.

power pumps on faucets, so late-night baths or showers may disturb them. If this is the case, site the bathroom next to the master bedroom. Teenagers will appreciate a shower room close to their bedrooms, so consider that if you're planning an attic. Older children consider it very grown up to have their bedrooms equipped with a small basin.

As parents, if you crave your own facilities, consider incorporating the main bathroom into the master bedroom. This is particularly effective in a loft space, or knocked-through, L-shaped bedrooms in an older house. The arrangement works best when children are small, so they can bathe while you sleep

LEFT AND ABOVE LEFT: The bigger your family, the more towel space you need. In addition to a heated towel rod, consider fun extras such as an Oriental-style bamboo ladder or folding wooden or chrome racks. A coat stand makes a great choice for bathrobes. OPPOSITE: In a traditional bathroom, experiment with less conventional storage options. A distressed wooden trunk can be filled with spare towels, and a glass- or chicken-wire-fronted cabinet makes a great display for attractive bath products, one shelf for each member of the family.

OPPOSITE LEFT, FROM ABOVE TO BELOW, AND RIGHT: Help everyone stay neat by furnishing the bathroom with plenty of large hooks for clothes, and occasional baskets for toilet paper, washcloths, or bathtime reading. In a large family, you might even consider numbered hooks to encourage order.
LEFT: It's possible to choose a sophisticated decorative scheme, whatever age the kids are. With a washable slipcover and easy-to-wipe paneling, this all-white bathroom is both practical and beautiful.

late and there's lots of space for running around. As parents, you get the benefit of a roomy, light bathroom for relaxing in before bed (but install sliding screens or double doors for privacy at night). The downside is you may find little ones passing through your room on midnight trips to the bathroom. Another solution is to formally separate the bathroom, but make it large enough for all the family. The ideal combination is a separate children's shower room and toilet as well.

Less-than-perfect plumbing should be overhauled. It's vital for busy families to have piping hot water that won't run out after the first bath. If moving house, invest in a new, larger hot-water tank, but make sure your boiler is powerful enough to keep it stocked. Power pumps will improve water flow from faucets and the shower head. Include at least one heated towel rod on the hot water circuit, to avoid endlessly soggy towels. Alternatively, an electrical one can be switched on when needed. Think about underfloor heating, as it makes even chilly stone floors cozy.

Storage is crucial. If the linen cupboard is in the bathroom, it's the obvious place to store towels. Otherwise, opt for a slim freestanding unit, built-in shelves, or deep drawers beneath a

vanity unit. Where do all the lotions and potions go? Allow the family one shelf above the basins for everyday bottles, from cleanser to aftershave, and wall-mount glasses, so small kids don't knock them over. Then insist that all remaining clutter is stowed away. Allocate an individual shelf or cupboard to each family member. A row of medicine-style cabinets or lockers looks trendy and neat. Inside one large cupboard, smaller containers can hold everything from hairbrushes to soaps. Don't forget a big laundry bin, and locate it in an obvious place, so kids actually use it.

When planning a bathroom from scratch, draw a floor plan to scale and move around cutouts of proposed sanitaryware. It's the only way to assure a free-flowing layout, allowing quick access to the toilet and basins in the morning. It will also help you make design choices. For example, if there's no room for a hinged shower door, plan a stationary sand-blasted screen. If possible, position the bathtub centrally rather than against the wall. It's easier to get at slippery small children, and may create a free corner where a chair can go.

When it comes to sanitaryware, nothing beats a big bathtub. Smaller siblings can share bathtime, and grown-ups enjoy the luxury, too. Cast-iron styles often come in extra-deep or long proportions, and traditional rolltop tubs are generously sized. Choose bath sides that won't spoil if splashed, such as painted board, laminate, or sand-blasted glass lit from within with colored lights. Centrally sited mixer

OPPOSITE, TOP ROW:
A traditional style of sanitaryware, teamed with a classic all-white scheme, makes the perfect family choice. It can be dressed up with pretty chandeliers, antique mirrors, or giant scented candles to suit grown-ups, but looks equally at home furnished with kids' bathtime toys, or a distressed wooden stool for little ones to reach the basin.

OPPOSITE, BOTTOM ROW:
Don't despair if the family bathroom is tiny. Look for fixtures that can double up, from a combined radiator and towel rod to a basin inset into a storage unit. If you have a family of teenagers, is a tub essential? A great power shower, which takes up less room, may be a better alternative.

BELOW, LEFT TO RIGHT:
Choose faucets and fixtures with practicality in mind. A generous-sized spout will fill a tub quicker than two conventional ones, while basin mixer faucets reduce the likelihood of younger kids scalding their hands.

faucets are more comfortable for children, and take up even less room if wall-mounted. And add an efficient shower head attachment, so hair-washing is possible even if the shower cubicle is in use.

Two basins will speed up morning ablutions. Wall-mounted ceramic styles take up less room than traditional pedestal basins, or double up on facilities by putting a basin on a stainless-steel stand, so towels can hang below. Alternatively, consider counter-sinking two basins into a built-in storage unit with cupboards beneath. In a contemporary bathroom, a purpose-built long, shallow, tiled or ceramic trough is a streamlined option. If the toilet is situated in the main bathroom, it's essential to have at least one other elsewhere in the house. And however sociable a bathroom you've planned, don't forget a lock on the door—well out of the reach of tiny fingers.

A shower is essential in a household containing teenagers. If possible, install a separate shower cubicle within the family bathroom, rather than making do with a shower head over the tub. Squeeze in a separate shower room elsewhere at home—even in the utility room or cellar—and you will immediately triple the family's washing options. Invest in the best shower you can afford, with a good shower head and a pump for excellent water pressure.

In a separate shower room, go for a wet-room style with tiled walls and a floor drain, so that younger kids can pile in together instead of squeezing into a small cubicle. Keep things streamlined with wall-mounted soap and shampoo dispensers. Flooring must be non-slip.

BELOW, LEFT TO RIGHT: If space is tight, investigate alternative options, including an extra-small bathtub, a sitz-style bath/shower, or one that is custom-built to fit the space and lined with tiles. A small tub can be comforting for little ones, but consider growing children and adults' needs, too, by combining it with a shower option. OPPOSITE: A wet-room-style shower, with floor drain, is quick, practical, and fun for kids.

OPPOSITE: Consider privacy in the family bathroom. No one wants to look directly at the toilet, and even little kids can be surprisingly prudish about sharing with older siblings. Conceal the toilet behind a discreet partition, or provide a sliding sand-blasted glass door.

ABOVE AND LEFT: If the bathroom is an odd shape, consider building bathing facilities to fit the available space. Mosaic tiles fit the tightest corners and make a great decorative choice, since they come in myriad bright colors, and can be used to individualize a room with unusual motifs and shapes.

Mosaic tiles or concrete are good options, but add a nonslip rubber or slatted wood mat on stone floors. Make the shower room fun and bright for the kids. Mosaic and ceramic tiles come in myriad strong colors, while cement can be inset with glitter mosaics or pebbles for the ultimate nonslip surface.

In contrast, the main bathroom needs a neutral color scheme, as one minute it will be filled with bright bath toys, the next needed as a preparty relaxation zone for teenagers or grown-ups. Paint walls in cool shades or choose a polished plaster finish or all-over tiling in pastel or white tiles—neutrals are soothing for everyone, and splashes are easily wiped down. Likewise, paneling or tongue and groove, painted with eggshell, are practical options. Pick flooring that is safe but robust. Stone, wood, or the ever-practical linoleum and rubber are all good choices and come in a variety of neutral shades. Control daylight with a simple shade, wooden shutters, or sand-blasted-glass panels in the windows.

Because the family bathroom is shared by all ages, try to include special treats everyone will enjoy. A cozy armchair, slipcovered in terrycloth, is the perfect spot for little ones cuddling up after a bath or teenagers painting their toenails. Provide plenty of fluffy towels, perhaps color-coding them for each member of the family. There should be a mirror that everyone can see into (and if kids are tiny, provide a sturdy stool), with good lighting for makeup. If you've a family of boys, add a shaver socket and extendable mirror. A chrome trolley, to hold magazines and comics, and a radio—so that everyone can sing along in the bath—should keep the whole family happy.

OPPOSITE AND RIGHT: If a parents' connecting bathroom is to be shared by all, great storage is essential. Include space for toiletries and clean towels, not to mention cleaning materials, toilet rolls, and medicine cabinet essentials. Look for extra-large towel rods (right) to accommodate multiple towels. Make the family bathroom cozy for everyone. Underfloor heating is ideal, while lighting on a dimmer and a low tub that small children will find easy to get into are desirable.

parents' rooms

Parents deserve a tranquil and relaxing bedroom, a retreat from the rigors and noise of family life. Children need to understand it's a private place, too. To create the ultimate adult switch-off zone, plan the master bedroom with cool colors and minimal furniture in mind. And don't forget to include the little luxuries so often edited out of a practical, family-friendly home. This is your space, so fill it with all the things you love best.

THIS PAGE AND OPPOSITE: If space is tight, there may barely be room in the parental bedroom for a double bed, let alone other furniture. Plan for this by devoting an entire wall to storage. A small room will look calmer if surfaces seamlessly blend into to one another, so white walls, closet doors, even bedlinen, are easy on the eye. Think about the ceiling. Just as babies need something stimulating to look at, don't exhausted parents deserve a tranquil patch for contemplation, from palest blue to *trompe l'oeil* clouds?

No adult, once a parent, will ever view the master bedroom in quite the same way again. It's no longer just a place to get dressed and to sleep. When your children are young, it's their first port of call from as early as daybreak, a focus for imaginative games, quiet cuddles, and TV-watching in the parental bed. And while on weekends you won't see older children for dust, it's still a sanctuary for them during times of illness or for evening chats. Yet perhaps its greatest significance for time-pressed parents is that it's a retreat, a place for me-time and for winding down.

In planning a family home from scratch, consider the potential of each bedroom before choosing your own. Many parents pick the largest room out of convention, but this may not be the best strategy. Think five years ahead—how will family life have moved on? It would be a shame to install a luxurious connecting shower room off the master bedroom, only to find two years later that siblings need a bigger room to share—in other words, yours! Could you bag a room under the eaves, with the potential for a walk-in closet, or would it be better divided into two small rooms plus shower room for soon-to-be teenagers?

Privacy is important. No one wants to ban kids from the bedroom, but it's good for them to understand that, just as you respect their rooms, so they should respect yours. This division

may be simply achieved in an apartment by locating your bedroom at one end of the corridor and the children's at the other. If you are building a house, and there's space, create a "buffer" zone between the bedroom door and the room where you sleep. A large room can be divided into a "suite" of bathroom, bedroom, and tiny dressing room, all leading off a short corridor that's accessed from one door.

Sometimes the parents' room opens directly off the main living space and becomes part of it during the day. This is common in an open-plan single-level area or in a small apartment, where every square inch counts. Create privacy with sliding doors in sand-blasted glass or painted board, or more traditional folding or double doors. All these options aid in noise control if the kids get up before you do. In a loft space, create cozy cubicle rooms for the children at ground

LEFT AND OPPOSITE: Whatever age your children are, it's worth considering the issue of privacy. So think about access routes to the bedroom. If the room is large, consider sectioning off the initial third (left), and furnish it with a small sofa or daybed, where children can congregate in the morning (or middle of the night) without totally disturbing your peace. A sliding door dividing the two will be less intimidating than a shut door for small kids.

OPPOSITE: The older children get, the more likely it is you'll reclaim your bedroom as a sanctuary. Floor space once necessary for little ones playing can now be filled with useful extras, from a sofa to a desk or bookcase. This is the time to indulge all those decorative whims you've held back on for so long. An all-white bedroom creates the ultimate relaxation zone.
RIGHT: Enjoy making a decorative focus out of family photographs, which can be casually grouped together, as here, or hung to cover an entire wall.

level, then build a separate mezzanine-level sleeping platform for grown-ups. A glass or steel balustrade, along with an enclosed staircase, are safety essentials if the children are small.

In the parental bedroom, carefully chosen minimal furniture will go a long way to keeping your mood serene, as well as freeing up floor space for active kids. If you have little ones who cuddle up in bed with you, consider investing in a spacious king-sized bed. It's a good idea to include a small sofa. Children can perch here for early-morning TV-viewing while you snooze, or crash on it at night if they are feeling lonely. Alternatively, choose a convertible sofa. If you don't have a spare room, guests can sleep in the kids' rooms, while the children use the sofa bed. And don't forget a bedside table, stacked with all the books you never get to read during the day.

The master bedroom also needs great storage, so tired parents can quickly put away their own stuff at night. In a contemporary interior, a wall of closet doors painted to match the walls hides everything. A pretty armoire or linen press are traditional options. Make good use of chainstore storage fixtures and kit out the inside with hanging rods, shelves, and baskets for smaller items. The easier it is for you to clear up, the less likely you are to drop a special dress on the floor late at night, only to find it fashioned into a "tent" in the morning.

Think of your bedroom as a second private living room. Yes, family life is sociable, but as children grow up, they no longer go to bed at 8:00; they will share most evenings with you, so it's nice to know you can retreat to your bedroom, good book in hand.

ABOVE, RIGHT, AND OPPOSITE: If you have rules about kids coming into the bedroom, make them clear from an early age, so everyone knows the limits. Guidelines might include no jumping on the bed, not dragging the covers off, and not investigating the contents of the closet (particularly in the case of teenagers!). But let them enjoy the luxuries you've chosen to surround yourself with, too. Children will enjoy a bit of grown-up glamour, be that a glittery canvas, touchy-feely textures on the bed, or a dresser with adjustable mirrors and tempting little drawers.

ABOVE LEFT, AND OPPOSITE: Given that the parental bedroom is all about relaxing, treat yourself to comfortable, even indulgent furnishings. Pile the bed high with feather pillows, invest in a good-quality mattress, and choose a padded fabric headboard to make the most of any (very occasional) sleep-ins. It's a good idea to have a selection of blankets as well as a cotton-covered comforter, so the whole family can enjoy a Sunday morning tucked up watching TV in bed.

ABOVE RIGHT: There are many advantages to deciding to site the parental bedroom in an attic. Apart from great natural light, there's the noise factor—no one thundering upstairs, and no patter of tiny feet overhead when you're trying to stay asleep. RIGHT: If there's no room to squeeze in a comfy sofa, an occasional chair, even in the tiniest of bedrooms, is still ideal for laying out tomorrow's clothes, helping a child get dressed, or impromptu nighttime chats.

Add a small television, and there will be no more arguments about who watches what. Think carefully about the atmosphere you want to create. Install dimmer switches on wall-mounted lights by the sofa and bed. Build in a stereo system if you can. Be indulgent. This is your private space, so if you want to fill a wall with your kids' artwork and family photos for contemplation in bed, do so.

The way you decorate the bedroom will crucially affect its ambience. It's refreshing to choose a moody color scheme—muted off-pastels, neutrals, or exotic shades like damson or chartreuse—in contrast to the whites and clear colors so typical of a family home. Experiment with abstract or metallic wallpapers, or more romantic *toile de Jouy*. And don't be afraid to indulge in luxurious textures, even if you do have small children. Silk curtains and velvet pillows are perfectly possible, as long as the kids are taught to treat them with respect. Better still, hunt out satin eiderdowns or woolen throws that are washable, or at least drycleanable. And be warned. All children, from toddlers to teenagers, are as tuned-in to luxury as we are. Blink twice and that devore velvet throw will be on its way upstairs, on route to a small person's bedroom.

outdoors

storage

traffic areas

practical zones

"The kids know there's a place for everything in the house. It's easier for them, because they know where to find things, and good for me—because I hate to tidy up!"

LENA, MOTHER

"Keep the right stuff in the right places. We can just reach under the kitchen benches and get to the Play-doh, rather than having to run upstairs to the kids' bedrooms."

SIMON, FATHER

"Storage and more storage! While the benefits of an open-plan space are that kids can play everywhere, I want to be able to tidy everything away at the end of the day."

CLAIRE, MOTHER

outdoors

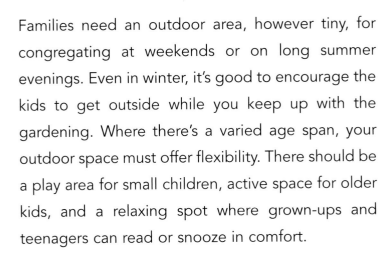

Families need an outdoor area, however tiny, for congregating at weekends or on long summer evenings. Even in winter, it's good to encourage the kids to get outside while you keep up with the gardening. Where there's a varied age span, your outdoor space must offer flexibility. There should be a play area for small children, active space for older kids, and a relaxing spot where grown-ups and teenagers can read or snooze in comfort.

TOP LEFT AND OPPOSITE: Create an indoor/outdoor room for family use, and it will rarely be empty. Guard against a variable climate by choosing a space that offers some protection from the elements. A conservatory extension or patio with permanent roof and one or two fixed side walls are both good options. Furniture choices can be more varied if a space is sheltered. Consider rattan, bamboo, or upholstered styles— more comfortable than conventional garden chairs. LEFT: The more seating choices around the house and garden, the better, from a balcony with rockers to a decked dining area.

The great outdoors is a vital extension to your family living space. We can't all enjoy big gardens, but when the sun comes out and the back door is open, even the tiniest patio comes into its own. Younger children are naturally attracted outside, needing little more than a stick or snail to entertain them, while computer-game-obsessed older siblings need a little more encouragement. What would make outdoors enjoyable for them? The simple addition of a football area or basketball hoop might do the trick. You may even discover a burgeoning gardener, in need of an experimental flowerbed.

Think about outdoor access. For smaller children, it's ideal if the kitchen/playroom opens directly onto the yard, so they can wander in and out under a watchful parental eye. In a contemporary home, floor-to-ceiling glass sliding doors, or those designed to fold back on themselves, will instantly double the available play space. In a more traditional home, French doors create a similar effect. For grown-ups and teenagers, consider the appeal of a planked "deck." Traditionally sited between indoors and an expanse of lawn, a deck is the perfect spot for lounging, so equip it with a rocking chair or (if the deck is covered with an awning) upholstered bench seats.

RIGHT: There are advantages to high enclosing walls in a small city yard: they can protect against flying footballs, provide privacy, and control noise. Prevent tall walls from overpowering a space and maximize light by painting walls in reflective pale colors or obscuring them with an energetic, robust flowering vine.

BELOW RIGHT: Everyone appreciates a cooling water feature, but if kids are small, install a cover for safety.
OPPOSITE: A playhouse needn't ruin an urban garden. Be inspired by the style of your house to create a purpose-built structure. Cement walls can be decorated with pebbles or handprints in abstract patterns.

Eating outdoors *en famille* is wonderfully sociable. Make it easy by having a table and chairs permanently set up, as impromptu lunches are less appealing if furniture must be moved first. Good-quality garden furniture designed to withstand the elements will last for more than a decade. Hardwood, aluminum, cast iron, and plastic are all good choices. Pick as large a table as possible, to accommodate any extra guests. Great extras include a big sun umbrella, a barbecue, and—the ultimate luxury—an outdoor heater for chillier nights.

When outdoor space is limited, it's important to combine practicality with good looks. Take the ages of your kids into account when choosing surfaces. If there are boys circling on bikes, forget grass—a tiny patch will soon become a mudbath. Instead, consider limestone paving or concrete, the ultimate roller-skating surface. Tiny children likely to take a tumble will fare better with decking. Concrete or brick walls, painted in strong Mediterranean shades or reflective white, can withstand repeated bashings from a football. If you have little ones or more considerate teenagers, woven willow or bamboo fence panels look good. Don't cut down on activity space by adding deep flowerbeds. Instead, group plants in containers, and ask the garden center to recommend child-friendly species.

BELOW: Whatever age your children are, accept that the yard will be infiltrated with equipment, from sit-on cars to scooters, bikes, and skateboards. Either include a shed, for quick clear-ups, or a covered outdoor "closet" in modern stainless steel for urban spaces, or seasoned hardwood in traditional yards. It can be softened with climbers or made funky with strings of plastic beads.

Having children needn't mean the end of a beautifully planned garden. For a start, most kids enjoy the process of gardening and will appreciate the chance to grow vegetables they can eat, flowers to pick for their bedrooms, and undergrowth to rummage in. Try to choose fast-growing shrubs or groundcover plants that can be trained to conceal the kids' play area, and if there's room, allow for an area of tall, robust grasses or a thicket of bamboo, which makes play much more fun.

Don't discount play equipment just because a space is small. Many outlets sell smaller-scale jungle gyms designed for urban spaces, while older kids will enjoy a wall-mounted basketball hoop or pop-up soccer goalposts. A small trampoline can be squeezed into a corner, but position it over a sunken area, filled with woodchips, if there's stone flooring elsewhere. If reclaiming the yard for adult barbecues is important, pick foldaway play equipment, and stash it in a small shed or storage bunker. Planning a garden from scratch allows for tasteful solutions. Consider an inset sandpile with a flush cover to match the decking, or a playhouse designed in the same materials as the walls/fence, so it seamlessly blends in.

If you have the luxury of a large yard, divide the space with multiple activities in mind. Older, active children benefit from space for ball games, but no one wants to view scuffed grass. Position the kickabout zone at the end of the yard, and screen it from the house using trellising, covered with a fast-growing creeper vine, or by planting large shrubs and flowering trees to conceal the area behind.

Provide an array of outdoor activities the whole family can enjoy. Specialized mail-order catalogs sell garden games from giant building blocks to chess; then there are the classics, such as croquet or quoits. Tomboys of either sex will enjoy a sturdy rope and tire securely fastened to a tree branch.

ABOVE: Building a wall to keep kids safe in the yard is a good idea, but make sure there is a door to the street so active kids arriving or departing on bikes or roller skates don't tread mud through the house.

RIGHT: In multifunctional family living spaces where kids are moving constantly in and out, pick furniture that looks good in both areas. Metal café-style furniture, low-slung plastic chairs, and hardwood benches are good examples.

OPPOSITE: Converted warehouse homes often boast substantial outdoor space, though it may be impossible to transform this into a leafy oasis. Instead, play up the industrial aspect with concrete flooring, a wooden bench on chains, and a skateboard ramp.

Also consider the option of larger outdoor play equipment. Specialized companies sell modular gyms that can be added to with ropes, scramble nets, swings, or slides. They are not cheap, but will entertain your kids for years, and are often manufactured in hardwoods to blend with the garden. Older children will relish a treehouse or other retreat. It's cheaper to buy a wooden shed and customize the interior than splashing out on a gingerbread-style playhouse that kids will soon grow out of. If the yard is large, a big shed, wired and plumbed, makes a great game room. Check planning restrictions first, though.

The older kids get, the more they value privacy—outdoors as well as in. Teenagers might want to study in the backyard in the warmer months, and adults need an outdoor escape. So in addition to sun loungers, provide fold-up canvas deckchairs or director's chairs that can be carried to the end of the backyard.

A big hammock will appeal to all age groups. More formal options include a painted wooden gazebo, a garden seat overhung with a vine or an upholstered swing chair. A summerhouse provides excellent out-of-season storage for everything from umbrellas to basebats.

For inner-city-dwellers, the only chance of outdoor space may be upward, on a roof terrace. If you have small kids, high fencing and easy access via a sturdy staircase are essentials. But while ball games are clearly out of the question, a wading pool and sandpile can easily be accommodated. If you have older children, turn the roof terrace into a trendy oasis. Add a small water feature—a fountain or a trickle of water over pebbles (avoid ponds if kids are still small). Invest in some funky molded-plastic outdoor furniture, lay a square of Astroturf, and string the surrounding balustrade with outdoor mini tree lights.

OPPOSITE AND THIS PAGE: The average roof terrace tends to be small, but if possible it's still worth dividing up the available space to suit several different functions. Most important is a generous table and chairs, as large as the space will allow. Also consider a trellis screen or bamboo or wicker fence panels to divide the eating area from a lounge spot in the sun. Exotic trees grown in containers can also create a pretty screen. Take time to plan your outdoor lighting—perfect for encouraging impromtu alfresco family meals.

Great storage is the backbone of a smooth-running family home. Plan it successfully, and it will help reduce (if not prevent) the amiable chaos of family life. The key to good storage is to have more than you think is necessary, because kids' gear multiplies daily. And plan it with a decorative eye. Storage is essential in every room of the house, so it should look great as well as being practical.

THIS PAGE: Built-in storage needn't mean a closet, and in a tiny room, they may not even be an option. So think laterally. In this teenager's bedroom, a high platform bed accommodates plenty of drawer space. And for kids in a hurry, clearing clothes and possessions into low-level drawers is often more user-friendly than a closet. A wall-mounted TV shelf also saves on floor space.

OPPOSITE, ABOVE, AND BELOW: Nothing beats cube shelves for quick toy storage, and—in later years—for stowing away books and CDs. Doors will hide messier items.

Nothing oils the wheels of family life better than a good storage system. Yet having ample, well-planned storage isn't just a question of owning a large house. A small living space works perfectly well if there's a place for everything. Family life isn't about having an immaculate home, but it isn't about living in chaos, either. It's harder to encourage kids to be neat if there's no designated storage for daily items. So be realistic. Aim for a storage system that allows for a good clear-up when there's time, and basic organization when there isn't.

The bigger your family, the more clutter there will be. And from babyhood on, it multiplies. Rule number one is to have regular clear-outs, especially at Christmas and birthdays, when there's an influx of new stuff. Rule number two is to have a clear idea of what must be stored, and how frequently it's used. Get children (and grown-ups) to list their essential stuff, from sports gear to CDs, camera equipment to blankets. Examine the available storage through the whole house, from the cellar to the bedrooms, then create a plan of where everything should go.

THIS PAGE AND OPPOSITE: In small spaces or restricted areas, it's imperative for storage to be "invisible," so it won't get in the way of kids running around or interfere with a sleek, contemporary interior. Flush doors with invisible touch catches, in a color or finish to match the walls, are the ideal option. A carefully planned visual break in a run of cabinets can house a TV, computer, breakfast bar, or work surface.

OPPOSITE, ABOVE FAR RIGHT: When storage conceals appliances such as a CD player or video, the need for ventilation can be turned into a decorative asset. Punched metal, trellized board, or cutout circles look stylish and are practical.

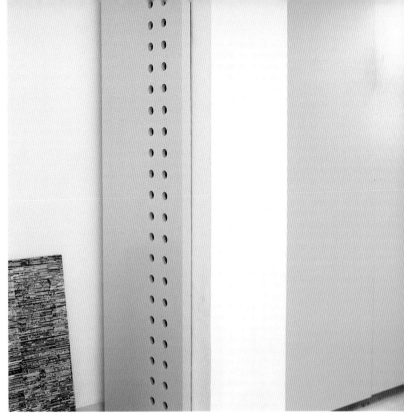

Contemplating the house in its entirety, rather than room by room, means things get stored logically. Why keep your son's sports gear in his room if it's easier to grab it in the hall?

Fitted made-to-measure storage is an investment, but it pays vast practical dividends. In a large room, with space to spare, you can't beat an uninterrupted bank of wall-to-wall shelves. But it's still possible to be inventive when space is tight. In a small room, "stealing" a depth of 20 inches across the width of one wall creates enough space for a wall of flush cupboards. Precisely because fitted storage is tailormade, it maximizes the available space in the most awkward of corners, from bookshelves above a door to vertical shoe-racks under the stairs. It can also be as task- or object-specific as you like. A run of minimalist storage cupboards can house the kids' TV, a contemporary playroom bench can conceal toys beneath its lid, and bulky items—from the vacuum cleaner to the space-hopper—can be squeezed into understair cupboards.

ABOVE LEFT AND RIGHT: Storage must fit in with your decorative style, so if your look is more traditional, pick simple mirrored or paneled freestanding armoires. Rethink the way you use classic pieces. A large armoire might do better service as a toy cupboard in the kitchen, rather than cluttering up a bedroom, while a chest of drawers on a roomy landing can house extra bedding.

LEFT: Experiment with the levels of shelving or open storage, especially in a small space. Shelves can be run around a room at ceiling height, hung below a window, or floor-mounted.

OPPOSITE, LEFT AND RIGHT: Tall, thin shelving units can serve kids' and adults' needs alike. Dangerous or precious items that you'd rather small children didn't reach, or infrequently used toys and books, can be stored well out of the way, while lower shelves are devoted to everyday necessities. A library ladder can be a fun addition for accessing very tall shelves.

How do you want storage to look? In rooms where you entertain, or want to feel peaceful, always have cabinet doors, so it doesn't matter if there's chaos lurking within. Flush-fitting doors painted or wallpapered to match walls will discreetly disappear, especially if they have invisible touch catches. For contrast, consider stainless steel, laminates, or gloss-painted board, or in traditional homes, paneled door fronts. In playrooms or utility zones, open shelves or wall-mounted cube storage are ideal since they provide instant access for kids. Keep them neat by using stylish containers in wicker, cardboard, or plastic.

If moving into a new house, don't rip out existing storage just because it looks dated. The original carcasses may be put to good use. Molded doors can be replaced with plastic or sand-blasted glass, and shelves made more contemporary with the addition of a thick front edge. If you're staying put in an existing house and can't afford built-in storage, consider off-the-shelf options. They are inexpensive and available in many finishes, from wood veneers to lacquer. These days, there's an array of unusual door handles that will customize cabinets further, but pick chunky versions if there are small kids around.

Not everyone wants sleek built-in storage. Freestanding pieces can move home with you, and have the potential to shift from one room to another as family needs alter. Regular furniture can also be customized. A beautiful armoire will be more user-friendly if it has many shelves, instead of a high hanging rod, while a low retro-style drinks cabinet could conceal the video. Kids will enjoy foraging in secondhand stores for a chest of drawers or bureau that they can paint and customize for their room. Also consider inexpensive chain-store storage options, from a TV cabinet to shoe cupboards. And get inventive with

THIS PAGE AND OPPOSITE: The average family accumulates an amazing amount of stuff, but organizing everything by type, rather than by owner, can help. For example, decide that all books are shelved in the living room, all outdoor gear stashed in the cellar, and all CDs kept in the kitchen, rather than distributed around the house. The more you can compartmentalize storage, the better. Thus, shelves should be equipped with lots of baskets, the inside of a cabinet with sliding drawers and metal racks, and the backs of doors with multiple, rather than single, hooks. And keep a roomy easy-to-carry basket permanently at the bottom of the stairs. Encourage anyone going up—from little ones to grown-ups—to replace stray items on a regular basis, and that way no one bears the brunt of a mass clear-up.

budget plywood or galvanized metal storage cubes or stacking storage systems from chain stores. Wall-mounted at unusual heights (from ankle level to above a window), or used in multiple quantities, they can look as chic as custommade storage.

All storage systems work best with containers that hold smaller items. You can't go wrong with clear plastic crates and lidded containers, clearly labeled, so kids can see toys and equipment at a glance. Grown-ups might prefer rattan baskets, zinc containers, or cardboard boxes, to hold everything from photos to Christmas decorations. Put kids' stuff on lower shelves and infrequently used items at the top. Don't clutter valuable cupboard space with out-of-season items. Banish them to the attic or the cellar. Make good use of ad hoc storage accessories, like wall-mounted CD, wine, and magazine racks. If there's a space for everything, then everyone— even the laziest child—can be persuaded to put things away.

However good the storage system, it's vital to provide the whole family with the means for a rapid clear-up when visitors are imminent or you have had enough of slowly encroaching chaos. Each room should have a basket, tucked out of sight, for magazines and toys. Hang hooks in bathrooms, halls, and kitchens, for getting everything off the floor quickly. And invest in an attractive filing cabinet, in powder-coated steel, to keep family paperwork under control.

Every parent knows the exuberance with which children arrive home, dump their stuff in the hall, and clatter up the stairs. All too often, these traffic areas don't get the attention they deserve. So treat such crucial spaces with respect. With robust surfaces and proper storage to keep them clutter-free, efficient traffic areas make for streamlined, safe family living. They can also become the most dramatic-looking areas of the house.

Every home needs an inviting hallway, to welcome family and visitors alike. So be strict with the kids about not dumping bags on the floor. Put pegs on the wall at varying levels and have several shoe racks, so hastily discarded gear can be immediately stowed. Wall-hang bikes on a pulley system, and fold strollers before storing them under the stairs. If there's room, add a bench so kids can boot up comfortably, and school gear be left out for the morning. If there's no space for a traditional hall table, wall-mount a large letter rack by the front door, so school notices and mail don't go astray, and add hooks for keys.

Stairs must be safe. If you move to a new house when kids are small, check there's no more than a 4-inch gap between bannisters and replace any worn, slippery stair carpet. Where stair gates are essential, rather than buy ugly white metal

OPPOSITE: Pay attention to entry and exit points, both practically and visually. Esthetically, it's pleasurable for everyone entering to see through to a vista outdoors. If there's no such view, might a doorway be moved to allow for one, or French doors positioned at the rear so kids can run straight outdoors? If there's space, it's a good idea to locate a powder room close to the front or back door.

LEFT AND BELOW: In a contemporary space, solid plywood, toughened glass, or metal mesh make sturdy alternatives to traditional bannisters and may be safer for small children to use.

BELOW LEFT AND OPPOSITE, RIGHT: In a big hall, one or two key pieces will set the decorative tone, but they must be practical, too. A bench or upholstered sofa is useful for school stuff, while a narrow hall table will hold all the paraphernalia. BELOW RIGHT AND OPPOSITE, LEFT: Putting built-in cabinets in an already narrow corridor hall may not be an obvious option, but the resulting storage will keep the precious remaining space clear.

versions, get a carpenter to create a simple design in wood, then paint to match the décor. Good lighting is essential. Inserting a skylight above the stairwell can flood it with light. Side lights, on a dimmer, at intervals on the stairs, will provide a welcome home to late-arriving teenagers. Low-voltage lights inset at ankle height can illuminate treads to a basement kitchen. Consider noise levels. Bare wood or zinc-clad stairs look great, but the clattering of noisy kids will upset neighbors.

Corridors also take a battering, from toddlers on trikes to the indoor roller-blading and football of older kids. Keeping corridors clutter-free makes life safer, and it's more fun for children—why shouldn't they skateboard indoors? Traditionally, ground-floor corridors double as a space to hang coats, but if the corridor is narrow, hunt elsewhere for a cloakroom. Basement entrances make a good spot, as does the back door area. Put up pegs and a storage unit, so each child has a place to stow his gear. Cylindrical containers can house basebats or tennis racquets, while rubber or galvanized troughs can hold outdoor shoes.

Decoratively speaking, easy-care practical surfaces are the key to good-looking traffic areas. However strict you are with the kids, small children always go upstairs with jammy hands trailing the wall, and boys inevitably kick a football around before

LEFT AND BELOW: Traffic areas need good lighting to transform them into cheerful, energetic zones and keep them safe. Swap gloomy single hanging fixtures overhead for low-voltage lights, which provide clear illumination, but install a dimmer switch, so that at night corridors and landings are still gently lit for late-arriving teenagers or sleepwalking children.

escaping to the park. So, given that halls and stairs are expensive to redecorate, choose wisely. Many interior designers swear by using abstract patterned wallpaper, since it won't show the inevitable scuffs. Painted paneling or tongue and groove always looks good. If painting in plain shades, choose muddy or deep tones in vinyl silk or eggshell, which has a wipe-clean finish.

Flooring also takes a severe battering. While 100% wool carpet cleans up well (choose a heavy traffic variety), sisal or coir are hard-wearing and often come in striped or heavily textured versions that don't show the dirt. If you can, put a stair carpet that starts above the level of the hall floor so that mud from careless feet won't be a problem. Limestone, ceramic tiles, parquet, or floorboards are all easily washed and can be successfully combined with underfloor heating.

Traffic areas deserve dramatic decorative attention. There's no point designing light-filled imaginative rooms if the linking corridors are dark and boring. Paint corridor walls in bright shades, or choose bold flooring, such as poured rubber in a strong color. Traffic areas are the ideal spot to display family ephemera that you, the kids, and guests will all enjoy looking at. Buy cheap wooden frames, paint them all the same color, then frame sports certificates, vacation photos, or great kids' artwork.

LEFT AND ABOVE: Try not to leave the hall and corridor walls plain and boring. If the rest of the house is decorated in all-white or neutral hues, ask the kids to pick several bright colors, and get them to help paint expanses of wall in their favorite energizing shades. Expanses of wall can be revitalized with mirrors to reflect light into dark corners, large-scale artist's canvases decked out in freehand stripes or dots, or a family tree hand-painted directly onto the wall.

resources

HOME FURNISHINGS FOR PARENTS
AND KIDS

ABC Carpet & Home
888 Broadway
New York, NY 10003
(212) 473-3000
Visit www.ABC.com for a retail outlet
near you.
Furnishings, linens, rugs, and other
accessories for the home.

Abodio
271 Pine Street
Seattle, WA 98101
(206) 343-3030
Desks, chairs, lighting, and storage
solutions.

Anthropologie
1700 Sansom Street, 6th floor
Philadelphia, PA 19103
Call (800) 309-2500 or visit
www.anthropologie.com for a store
near you.
Funky one-of-a-kind accessories,
furniture, hardware, rugs, and drapes.

Arroyo Design
224 North Fourth Avenue
Tucson, AZ 85705
(602) 884-1012
Home office furniture as well as other
home furnishings.

Bed, Bath & Beyond
620 Avenue of the Americas
New York, NY 10011
Call (212) 255-3550 or visit
www.bedbathandbeyond.com for a
store near you.
Everything for the bed and bath, plus
kitchen utensils, home décor, and
storage solutions.

Blackwelders
Call (800) 438-0201 or visit
www.homefurnish.com/blackwelders
for a retailer near you.
Beds and other home furnishings.

Crate & Barrel
646 N. Michigan Avenue
Chicago, IL 60611
(800) 996-9960
Visit www.crateandbarrel.com for a
store near you.
Good-value furniture and accessories,
from simple white china and glass to
dining room sets and beds for the
whole family.

Ethan Allen
Ethan Allen Drive
P.O. Box 1966
Danbury, CT 06813
Call (800) 228-9229 or visit
www.ethanallen.com for a
store near you.
Furniture for the home, including
bedroom, home office, and even
outdoor furniture.

For Mercy's Sake
3911 Kandy Drive
Austin, TX 78749
(512) 892-2077
Children's furniture.

Gloria's KidsBeds
1800 Post Road East
Westport, CT 06430
(888) 600-5437
Children's furniture, from bunk
beds to toy boxes.

IKEA
1800 East McConnor Parkway
Schaumburg, IL 60173
Call (800) 434-4532 or visit
www.ikea.com for a store near you.
Simple but well-designed furniture
you have to assemble yourself, plus
inexpensive storage and kitchenware.

Jennifer Convertibles
3302–3304 M Street NW
Washington, D.C. 20007
Call (202) 333-0080 or visit
www.jenniferfurniture.com for a store
near to you.
Sleeper sofas, armchairs, and rugs.

Little Colorado, Inc.
4450 Lipan Street
Denver, CO 80211
(303) 964-3212
Children's furniture.

Maine Cottage Furniture
P.O. Box 935
Yarmouth, ME 04096
(207) 846-7050
www.mainecottage.com
Simple furniture for every room of the
house.

Pier One Imports
71 Fifth Avenue
New York, NY 10003
Call (212) 206-1911 or visit
www.pier1.com for a store near you.
Home accessories, furniture (indoor
and out) from all over the world.

Pottery Barn
600 Broadway
New York, NY 10012
Call (800) 922-5507 or visit
www.potterybarn.com for a
store near you.
Quality furniture and accessories for
the home.

Target
800 Nicollet Mall
Minneapolis, MN 55403
Call (612) 338-0085 for a store near
you.
Affordable home furnishings, including
bed, bath, and kitchen supplies.

Urban Outfitters
Broadway & Bleeker
628 Broadway
New York, NY 10012
Call (212)475-0009 or visit
www.urbanoutfitters.com for
a store near you.
Trendy and fun home accessories
from candleholders to rugs to
beanbag chairs.

Wildzoo Furniture
63025 O.B. Riley Road #9
Bend, OR 97701
(888) 543-8588
Children's furniture.

Workbench
470 Park Avenue South
New York, NY 10016
Call (800) 380-2370 or visit
www.workbenchfurniture.com for a
store near you.
Clean and functional modern furniture
for bedrooms, eating, and living
rooms, storage and more.

STORAGE

California Closets
Call (888) 336-9797 or visit
www.calclosets.com for a
store near you.
As their slogan says, "Life, stuff,
storage."

Furniture at Work
517 South Lamar Boulevard
Austin, TX 78704
(512) 445-7001
Home office and storage solutions.

Hold Everything
1309-1311 Second Avenue
New York, NY 10021
Call (212) 879-1450 or visit
www.holdeverything.com for a store
near you.
Everything for storage, from baskets
to racks to shelves.

**Pressman Design Studio/Home
Suite Office**
271 Miller Road
East Greenbush, NY 12061
(518) 479-0012
Home office and storage solutions.

HARDWARE

The Antique Hardware Store
19 Buckingham Plantation Drive
Bluffton, SC 29910
(800) 422-9982
Unusual and antique hardware.

Home Depot
Visit www.homedepot.com for
a store near you.
A wide selection of hardware, paint,
lumber, kitchen installations, and
outdoor furniture.

Kohler Co.
Call (800) 456-4537 or visit
www.kohlerco.com
Kitchen furniture, plumbing, and sinks.

Restoration Hardware
935 Broadway
New York, NY 10011
(212) 260-9479
Visit www.restorationhardware.com for
a store near you.
Fine hardware, home furnishings,
lighting, and other accessories.

LIGHTING

Boyd Lighting
944 Folsom Street
San Francisco, CA 94107
(415) 778-4300

Brass Light Gallery
131 South First Street
Milwaukee, WI 53204
(800) 243-9595

Details
214 Durham Drive
Athens, AL 35611
(800) 833-0411

Hafele America Co.
3901 Cheyenne Drive
Archdale, NC 27263
(800) 334-1873

KITCHENWARE AND TABLEWARE

Fishs Eddy
869 Broadway
New York, NY 10011
Call (212) 420-2090 for other
locations.
Overstock supplies of simple mugs,
plates, bowls, and other tableware.

Tabletools
85 Furniture Row
Milford, CT 06460
(888) 211-6603
www.tabletools.com
Well-designed kitchen- and tableware.

Williams-Sonoma
121 East 59th Street
New York, NY 10022
Call (800) 541-1262 or visit
www.williams-sonomainc.com for a
store near you.
Cooking utensils and tableware.

BED AND BATH ACCESSORIES

The Company Store
301 Sky Harbour Drive
I-90, French Island Exit
LaCrosse, WI 54603
(800) 323-8000
www.thecompanystore.com
Online retailer of accessories for
bedroom and bath.

Gallery Linens
125 Main Street
Westport, CT 06880
(203) 222-8900
Linen supplier.

Gracious Home
1220 Third Avenue
New York, NY 10021
(212) 517-6300
www.gracioushome.com
Bedding, linens, and accessories.

Lassiter's Bed n' Boudoir
3500 Peachtree Road
Atlanta, GA 30326
(404) 261-0765
Accessories for the bed and bath.

Levine Linens
15 East Glenn Drive
Phoenix, AZ 85020
(602) 944-2898
Linen supplier.

Ralph Lauren Home Collection
1185 Sixth Avenue
New York, NY 10036
For a store in your area, call
(800) 377-POLO.
Linens, tableware, and towels.

Wamsutta
Spring Industries Inc.
P.O. Box 70
Fort Mill, SC 29716
Call (800) 931-1488 or visit
www.wamsutta.com for a retail
outlet near you.
A wide range of linens.

FABRICS AND WINDOW TREATMENTS

Hancock Fabrics
2605A West Main Street
Tupelo, MS 38801
(662) 844-7368
www.hancockfabrics.com
America's largest fabric store.

Laura Ashley Home Store
171 East Ridgewood Avenue
Ridgewood, NJ 07450
(201) 670-0688
Visit www.laura-ashleyusa.com for a
store near you.
Floral, striped, checked, and solid
cotton fabrics in a wide range of colors.

Smith + Noble
Corona, CA
(800) 560-0027
www.smithandnoble.com
Online store sells custom-made but
affordable window treatments, rugs,
pillows, slipcovers, and duvet covers.

Waverly
Call (800) 423-5881 or visit
www.waverly.com for a retail outlet
near you.
Window treatments, floor coverings,
fabric, and furniture.

PAINTS

Benjamin Moore & Company
51 Chestnut Ridge Road
Montvale, NJ 07645
(800) 826-2623

Janovic
1150 Third Avenue
New York, NY 10021
(800) 772-4381
www.janovic.com
Quality paints in a wide
range of colors.

**Martha Stewart Paint Collection
At Kmart**
Call (888) 627-8429 or visit
www.bluelight.com to find a
store near you.
A wide selection of decorative colors
that mix and match with Martha
Stewart's bedding, towels, and other
housewares.

Old Fashioned Milk Paint Co.
436 Main Street
P.O. Box 222
Groton, MA 01450
(478) 448-6336
www.milkpaint.com
These paints replicate the color and
finish of Colonial and Shaker antiques.

Pittsburgh Paints
1PPG Place
Pittsburgh, PA 15252
(888) 774-1010

Sherwin Williams
101 Prospect Street
Cleveland, OH 44115
(800) 622-8468

OUTDOORS

Gardener's Eden
P.O. Box 7307
San Francisco, CA 94120
Call (800) 822-9600 to mail order or
for a retailer near you.
Quality garden accessories and
furnishings for outdoors.

Smith & Hawken
2 Arbor lane
P.O. Box 6900
Florence, KY 41022
Call (800) 776-3336 or visit
www.smith-hawken.com for a retailer
near you.
This primarily mail-order store carries a
wide variety of garden furniture,
ornaments and accessories.

Swings N' Things
23052 Lake Forest Drive
Laguna Hills, CA 92653
(949) 770-7799
www.swingsandthingsca.com
Manufacture of premium-quality
playground equipment for the
backyard and home.

Walpole Woodworkers
767 East Street
Walpole, MA 02081
(800) 343-6948
Well-crafted garden furniture.

The Wicker Works
267 Eighth Street
San Francisco, CA 94103
Call (415) 626-6730 for a location near
you.
Outdoor furnishings in materials
from wicker to teak.

picture credits

All photography by Debi Treloar (unless stated otherwise)
Key: a=above, b=below, r=right, l=left, c=center.

1 Imogen Chappel's home in Suffolk; 2 Paul Balland and Jane Wadham of jwflowers.com's family home in London; 3 A family home in Manhattan, designed by architect Amanda Martocchio and Gustavo Martinez Design; 4 Kristiina Ratia and Jeff Gocke's family home in Norwalk, Connecticut; 5 New-build house in Notting Hill designed by Seth Stein Architects; 8 al Architect Simon Colebrook's home in London; 8 ac & br House by Knott Architects in London; 8 ar & bc Family home, Bankside, London; 8 cl Sarah Munro and Brian Ayling's home in London; 8 c Ian Hogarth's family home; 8 cr & bl A family home in London; photographs by Erwin Wurm; 9 House by Knott Architects in London; 10 a A Fifth Avenue Residence, New York City designed by Bruce Bierman Design, Inc.; 10 b Paul Balland and Jane Wadham of jwflowers.com's family home in London; 11 Imogen Chappel's home in Suffolk; 12–13 Kristiina Ratia and Jeff Gocke's family home in Norwalk, Connecticut; 14-15 Architect Simon Colebrook's home in London; 16-17 Kate and Dominic Ash's home in London; 18-19 New-build house in Notting Hill designed by Seth Stein Architects; 20 A family home in West London; 21 Catherine Chermayeff & Jonathan David's family home in New York, designed by Asfour Guzy Architects; 22-23 A family home in Manhattan, designed by architect Amanda Martocchio and Gustavo Martinez Design; 24-25 Imogen Chappel's home in Suffolk; 26 a Family home, Bankside, London; 26 b Ian Hogarth's family home; 27 A Fifth Avenue Residence, New York City designed by Bruce Bierman Design, Inc.; 28 Robert Elms and Christina Wilson's family home in London; 29 The Swedish Chair—Lena Renkel Eriksson; 30 a A family home in West London; 30 b Catherine Chermayeff & Jonathan David's family home in New York, designed by Asfour Guzy Architects; 31 The Swedish Chair—Lena Renkel Eriksson; 32 A family home in West London; 33 A family home in London; photographs by Erwin Wurm; 34-37 al Catherine Chermayeff & Jonathan David's family home in New York, designed by Asfour Guzy Architects; 37 c Robert Elms and Christina Wilson's family home in London; 37 b Paul Balland and Jane Wadham of jwflowers.com's family home in London; 37 ar Sarah Munro and Brian Ayling's home in London; 38-39 A family home in London; portraits by artist Julian Opie, Lisson Gallery; 40-41 Sarah Munro and Brian Ayling's home in London; paintings by Brian Ayling; 42-43 A family home in Manhattan, designed by architect Amanda Martocchio and Gustavo Martinez Design; 44-45 Jill Henry & Jon Pellicoro's family home in New York. Artwork by Jon Pellicoro; 46 A family home in Manhattan, designed by architect Amanda Martocchio and Gustavo Martinez Design; 47 Catherine Chermayeff & Jonathan David's family home in New York, designed by Asfour Guzy Architects; 48-49 House by Knott Architects in London; 50-51 A family home in London; 52 al Imogen Chappel's home in Suffolk; 52 acl A family home in Manhattan, designed by architect Amanda Martocchio and Gustavo Martinez Design; 52 bl A family home in West London; 52 ar Catherine Chermayeff & Jonathan David's family home in New York, designed by Asfour Guzy Architects; 52 cl Robert Elms and Christina Wilson's family home in London; 52 br The Swedish Chair—Lena Renkel Eriksson; 53 al Robert Elms and Christina Wilson's family home in London; 53 acl Kate and Dominic Ash's home in London; 53 acr A Fifth Avenue Residence, New York City designed by Bruce Bierman Design, Inc.; 53 ar Imogen Chappel's home in Suffolk; 53 b Paul Balland and Jane Wadham of jwflowers.com's family home in London; 54 Robert Elms and Christina Wilson's family home in London; 55 a Jill Henry & Jon Pellicoro's family home in New York. Artwork by Jon Pellicoro; 55 br Ian Hogarth's family home; 55 bl Catherine Chermayeff & Jonathan David's family home in New York, designed by Asfour Guzy Architects; 56-57 Kate and Dominic Ash's home in London; 58 l Kristiina Ratia and Jeff Gocke's family home in Norwalk, Connecticut; 58 ar A family home in West London; 58 br Sarah Munro and Brian Ayling's home in London; 59 a A family home in London; 59 b Architect Simon Colebrook's home in London; 60 al New-build house in Notting Hill designed by Seth Stein Architects; 60 ac Fifth Avenue Residence, New York City designed by Bruce Bierman Design, Inc.; 60 ar Ian Hogarth's family home; 60 cl Imogen Chappel's home in Suffolk; 60 c & bc A family home in West London; 60 cr Sarah Munro and Brian Ayling's home in London; paintings by Brian Ayling; 60 bl & br Robert Elms and Christina Wilson's family home in London; 61 A family home in West London; 62 a Catherine Chermayeff & Jonathan David's family home in New York, designed by Asfour Guzy Architects; 62 b Kate and Dominic Ash's home in London; 63 Ian Hogarth's family home; 64 & 65 b House by Knott Architects in London; 65 a Kate and Dominic Ash's home in London; 66 A family home in Manhattan, designed by architect Amanda Martocchio and Gustavo Martinez Design; 67 Family home, Bankside, London; 68 Paul Balland and Jane Wadham of jwflowers.com's family home in London; 69 Catherine Chermayeff &

Jonathan David's family home in New York, designed by Asfour Guzy Architects; 70-71 New-build house in Notting Hill designed by Seth Stein Architects; 72-73 A family home in West London; 74 al Imogen Chapel's home in Suffolk; 74 acl & b Ian Hogarth's family home; 74 ar House by Knott Architects in London; 75 al & ar Kristiina Ratia and Jeff Gocke's family home in Norwalk, Connecticut; 75 acl & cr New-build house in Notting Hill designed by Seth Stein Architects; 75 acr & bl Imogen Chapel's home in Suffolk; 75 br Kate and Dominic Ash's home in London; 76 al Kristiina Ratia and Jeff Gocke's family home in Norwalk, Connecticut; 76 ar Imogen Chapel's home in Suffolk; 76 b Sarah Munro and Brian Ayling's home in London; paintings by Brian Ayling; 77 Kristiina Ratia and Jeff Gocke's family home in Norwalk, Connecticut; 78 b Robert Elms and Christina Wilson's family home in London; 79 A family home in London; 80-81 Catherine Chermayeff & Jonathan David's family home in New York, designed by Asfour Guzy Architects; 82-83 Paul Balland and Jane Wadham of jwflowers.com's family home in London; 84-85 Kristiina Ratia and Jeff Gocke's family home in Norwalk, Connecticut; 86 al A family home in Manhattan, designed by architect Amanda Martocchio and Gustavo Martinez Design; 86 ac & ar A family home in West London; 86 cl The Swedish Chair—Lena Renkel Eriksson; 86 bl A Fifth Avenue Residence, New York City designed by Bruce Bierman Design, Inc.; 86 br Kate and Dominic Ash's home in London; 87 l A family home in Manhattan, designed by architect Amanda Martocchio and Gustavo Martinez Design; 87 c A Fifth Avenue Residence, New York City designed by Bruce Bierman Design, Inc.; 87 r Robert Elms and Christina Wilson's family home in London; 88-89 House by Knott Architects in London; 90 Family home, Bankside, London; 91 Ian Hogarth's family home; 92-93 New-build house in Notting Hill designed by Seth Stein Architects; 94 a Imogen Chappel's home in Suffolk; 94 b A family home in West London; 95 Robert Elms and Christina Wilson's family home in London; 96-97 Architect Simon Colebrook's home in London; 98-99 New-build house in Notting Hill designed by Seth Stein Architects; 100-101 Kristiina Ratia and Jeff Gocke's family home in Norwalk, Connecticut; 102 Sarah Munro and Brian Ayling's home in London; paintings by Brian Ayling; 103 Ian Hogarth's family home; 104 al Imogen Chappel's home in Suffolk; 104 ar & b The Swedish Chair—Lena Renkel Eriksson; 105 Catherine Chermayeff & Jonathan David's family home in New York, designed by Asfour Guzy Architects; 106 al & br A family home in West London; 106 ac, cl & c Kristiina Ratia and Jeff Gocke's family home in Norwalk, Connecticut; 106 ar Architect Simon Colebrook's home in London; 106 bl New-build house in Notting Hill designed by Seth Stein Architects; 106 bc & 107 House by Knott Architects in London; 108 a Architect Simon Colebrook's home in London; 108 b A family home in West London; 110-111 Kristiina Ratia and Jeff Gocke's family home in Norwalk, Connecticut; 112-113 New-build house in Notting Hill designed by Seth Stein Architects; 114 br House by Knott Architects in London; 115 a Sarah Munro and Brian Ayling's home in London; 115 b Family home, Bankside, London; 116 Architect Simon Colebrook's home in London; 117 House by Knott Architects in London; 118-119 Catherine Chermayeff & Jonathan David's family home in New York, designed by Asfour Guzy Architects; 120 a Ian Hogarth's family home; 120 b & 121 Catherine Chermayeff & Jonathan David's family home in New York, designed by Asfour Guzy Architects; 122 & 123 br Kate and Dominic Ash's home in London; 123 a New-build house in Notting Hill designed by Seth Stein Architects; 123 bl Architect Simon Colebrook's home in London; 124 & 125 ar Family home, Bankside, London; 125 al New-build house in Notting Hill designed by Seth Stein Architects; 125 b Ian Hogarth's family home; 126 al The Swedish Chair—Lena Renkel Eriksson; 126 ar Sarah Munro and Brian Ayling's home in London; 126 b & 127 l Family home, Bankside, London; 127 r A family home in Manhattan, designed by architect Amanda Martocchio and Gustavo Martinez Design; 128 al Catherine Chermayeff & Jonathan David's family home in New York, designed by Asfour Guzy Architects; 128 ac Kate and Dominic Ash's home in London; 128 ar, c & br The Swedish Chair—Lena Renkel Eriksson; 128 bl Family home, Bankside, London; 129 al & acl Kate and Dominic Ash's home in London; 129 ar Catherine Chermayeff & Jonathan David's family home in New York, designed by Asfour Guzy Architects; 129 c Imogen Chappel's home in Suffolk; 129 b Robert Elms and Christina Wilson's family home in London; 130 b A family home in West London; 131 Sarah Munro and Brian Ayling's home in London; 132 a Paul Balland and Jane Wadham of jwflowers.com's family home in London; 132 b Architect Simon Colebrook's home in London; 133 House by Knott Architects in London; 134 al A family home in Manhattan, designed by architect Amanda Martocchio and Gustavo Martinez Design; 134 ar & br House by Knott Architects in London; 134 bl The Swedish Chair—Lena Renkel Eriksson; 135 l Jill Henry & Jon Pellicoro's family home in New York; 135 r Kristiina Ratia and Jeff Gocke's family home in Norwalk, Connecticut; 136 l & br Ian Hogarth's family home; 136 ar & 137 b Family home, Bankside, London; 137 a A Fifth Avenue Residence, New York City designed by Bruce Bierman Design, Inc.; 144 House by Knott Architects in London.

architects and designers whose work is featured in this book:

Asfour Guzy Architects
594 Broadway
New York, NY 10012
t. (212) 334-9350
email: easfour@asfourguzy.com
Pages 21, 30 b, 34–37 al, 47, 52 ar, 55 br, 62 a, 69, 80–81, 105, 118–119, 120 b, 121, 128 al, 129 ar

Also involved in this project:
Cutting Edge Construction
71 Hudson Ave
Brooklyn, NY 11201
t/f. (718) 965-3027

Dominic Ash
Unit 7 Links Yard
29 Spelman Street
London E1 5LQ
t. +44 (20) 7377 1982
email: dominic@dominicash.co.uk
www.dominicash.co.uk
Pages 16–17, 53 acl, 56–57, 62 b, 65 a, 75 br, 86 br, 122, 123 br, 128 ac, 129 al & acr

Brian Ayling, Artist
t. +44 (20) 8802 9853
Pages 8 cl, 37 ar, 40–41, 58 br, 60 cr, 76 b, 102, 115 a, 126 ar, 131

Bruce Bierman Design, Inc.
29 West 15 Street
New York, NY 10011
t. (212) 243-1935
f. (212) 243-6615
www.biermandesign.com
Pages 10 a, 27, 53 acr, 60 ac, 86 bl, 87 c, 137 a

Imogen Chappel
+ 44
07803 156 081
Pages 1, 11, 24-25, 52 al, 53 ar, 60 cl, 74 al, 75 acr & bl, 76 ar, 94 a, 104 al, 129 c

Simon Colebrook, Architect
Douglas Stephen Partnership

140–142 St John Street
London EC1V 4UB
t. +44 (20) 7336 7884
f. +44 (20) 7336 7841
email: dsp@dspl.co.uk
www.dspl.co.uk

Also involved in this project:
Packman WCAS Engineers
BDA Quantity Surveyors
Pages 8 al, 14–15, 59 b, 96–97, 106 ar, 108 a, 116, 123 bl, 132 b

Dive Architects
10 Park Street
London SE1 9AB
t. +44 (20) 7407 0955
email: mail@divearchitects.com
www.divearchitects.com
Pages 8 ar & bc, 26 a, 67, 90, 115 b, 124, 125 ar, 126 b, 127 l, 128 bl, 136 ar, 137 b

Gustavo Martinez Design
206 Fifth Avenue
4th Floor
New York NY 10010
t. (212) 686-3102
f. (212) 686-3104
email: gmdecor@aol.com
Pages 3, 22–23, 42–43, 46, 52 acl, 66, 86 al, 87 l, 127 r, 134 al

jwflowers.com
Unit E8 & 9
1–45 Durham Street
London SE11 5JH
t. +44 (20) 7735 7771
f. +44 (20) 7735 2011
email: jane@jwflowers.com
www.jwflowers.com
Pages 2, 10 b, 37 b, 53 b, 82–83, 132 a

Knott Architects
98b Tollington Park
London N4 3RB
t. +44 (20) 7263 8844
f. +44 (20) 7263 4700

email: mail@knottarchitects.co.uk
www.knottarchitects.co.uk
Pages 8 ac & br, 9, 48–49, 64, 65 b, 74 ar, 88–89, 106 bc, 107, 114 br, 117, 134 ar & br

Kristiina Ratia Designs
t. (203) 852-0027
Pages 4, 12–13, 58 l, 75 al & ar, 76 al, 77, 84–85, 100–101, 106 ac, cl & c, 110–111, 135 r

Littman Goddard Hogarth
12 Chelsea Wharf
15 Lots Road
London SW10 9AS
t. +44 (20) 7351 7871
f. +44 (20) 7351 4110
email: info@lgh-architects.co.uk
www.lgh-architects.co.uk
Pages 8 c, 26 b, 55 bl, 60 ar, 63, 74 acl & b, 91, 103, 120a, 125 b, 136 l & br

Amanda Martocchio, Architect
189 Brushy Ridge Road
New Canaan, CT 06840
Pages 3, 22–23, 42–43, 46, 52 acl, 66, 86 al, 87 l, 127 r, 134 al

Musa
31 Holland Street
London W8 4NA
t. +44 (20) 7937 6282
A source of antique chandeliers and Venetian mirrors plus contemporary designer labels and vintage clothing
Pages 20, 30 a, 32, 52 bl, 58 ar, 60 c & bc, 61, 72–73, 74 acr, 86 ac & ar, 94 b, 106 al & br, 108 b, 130 b

Jon Pellicoro, Artist
email: mhfny@inch.com
Pages 44–45, 55 a, 68, 135 l

Nico Rensch
Architeam

www.architeam.co.uk
Pages 8 cr & bl, 33, 38-39, 50-51, 59 a, 79

Seth Stein Architects
15 Grand Union Centre
West Row
Ladbroke Grove
London W10 5AS
t. +44 (20) 8968 8581
f. +44 (20) 8968 8591
www.sethstein.com
Pages 5, 18–19, 60 al, 70–71, 75 acl & cr, 92–93, 98–99, 106 bl, 112–113, 123 a, 125 al, 133

The Swedish Chair
t. +44 (20) 8657 8560
email: lena@theswedishchair.com
www.theswedishchair.com
Pages 29, 31, 52 br, 86 cl, 104 ar & b, 126 al, 128 ar, c & br, 134 bl

Also involved in this project:
David Sandstrom, Painter
Decorative paintings and murals
t. +46 90 98049

Cecilie Telle, Knitted Felt Designer
email: cecilietelle@hotmail.com
www.amimono.demon.co.uk
Pages 8 ac & br, 9, 48–49, 64, 65 b, 74 ar, 88–89, 106 bc, 107, 114 br, 117, 134 ar & br

Christina Wilson, Interiors Stylist
email: christinawilson@btopenworld.com
Pages 28, 37 c, 52 cl, 53 al, 54, 60 bl & br, 78 b, 87 r, 95, 129 b

Thanks also to:
Heiberg Cummings Design
548 West 28th Street # 510
New York, NY 10001
t. (212) 239-4470
f. (212) 239-4830
email: WCummings@hcd3.com
www.hcd3.com

index

acknowledgments

Thank you, Alison Starling and David Peters of Ryland Peters & Small, for asking me to write a book devoted to family living, a subject close to my heart! Thanks to Annabel Morgan, for being an impeccable editor, and to Fiona Lindsay of Limelight Management, for her enthusiastic support. Thanks also to Gabriella Le Grazie and Fiona Walker, for vibrant art direction, and to Claire Hector for so efficiently sourcing great locations.

Thank you, Debi Treloar, for such fresh and beautiful photographs, which perfectly capture the essence of kids at home. And to all the families who invited us into their busy but beautiful private spaces, so the rest of us can be inspired!

Thanks to my parents Harry and Ann, and my sister, Sally, for making my first taste of family life such fun. But especially, thanks to Anthony, Cicely, and Felix, because we've had the best time creating our own family home, be it tidy, messy, or somewhere in between.